BLACK BAPTIST
SECONDARY SCHOOLS
IN VIRGINIA,
1887-1957

A Study in
Black History
by
LESTER F. RUSSELL

The Scarecrow Press, Inc.
Metuchen, N.J., & London
1981

Library of Congress Cataloging in Publication Data

Russell, Lester F   1919-
    Black Baptist secondary schools in Virginia,
1887-1957.

    Bibliography: p.
    Includes indexes.
    1. Afro-Americans--Education (Secondary)--
Virginia--History. 2. Afro-American Baptists--
Education (Secondary)--Virginia--History.
I. Title.
LC2802.V8R87   373. 755   80-22414
ISBN 0-8108-1373-4

DEDICATION

This book is dedicated to the men and women who pioneered to remove from Blacks the cloak of ignorance that was draped on them by more than two hundred and fifty years of slavery.

Particular tribute is paid to my parents, Reverend and Mrs. George Stephen Russell. They were both avowed Christians, with a firm belief in the power of the Almighty God to save souls, and education to liberate minds.

ACKNOWLEDGMENTS

The author is very grateful for the invaluable assistance given by many persons in the preparation of this book. Especial gratitude must go to Dr. James E. Wheeler, Associate Dean of the Graduate School of Education, Rutgers University, New Brunswick, New Jersey, and Dr. Samuel D. Proctor, Professor of Education at the same institution, for advising me to write on this highly significant topic.

I am also indebted to the late Drs. Marcus Ellison, President Emeritus of Virginia Union University, Richmond, and William L. Ransome, Pastor Emeritus of the First Baptist Church in South Richmond. Both gentlemen spent considerable time with me imparting knowledge on the secondary schools with which they were acquainted, with particular emphasis placed on how the schools were founded.

Finally, much credit is to be given to my very own tolerant and understanding wife, Mamie, who, throughout the research period, endured my agony, shared my anxiety, and encouraged me to persevere in concluding the study.

FOREWORD

The experience of Black Americans is unique in history. Their condition of bondage, their removal from their indigenous habitation, their cultural estrangement in North America, the prohibitions against their education, the blatant disregard of their family ties, and the long duration of their subjugation caused their quest for integration into the dominant society to stand as unprecedented in the world. Yet, in spite of it all, they are unrelenting in this quest and have rejected all notions of a separate or an inferior status.

One of the factors responsible for the persistence of this movement was the education that Blacks were able to receive, partly from the missionaries from the North and, to a large extent, education that they provided for themselves. This schooling gave them survival capacity, the skills, the language facility, the feeling of dignity, and the leadership cadre that they needed.

The effort was heroic, the challenge was momentous, and the obstacles and impediments were boundless. The story of the transformation of ex-slaves from wandering bands of penniless paupers to craftsmen, homeowners, teachers, social workers, ministers, physicians, lawyers, and politicians is one of the most miraculous metamorphoses that has ever taken place, comparable to Alexander's marches to the East, the Goths being brought into the Roman Empire, or Gandhi's liberation of India.

Dr. Russell has skillfully recorded for us one highly significant chapter of that record, the story of the secondary schools established by Blacks in Virginia. It is a microscopic view of a vast terrain, the circumference of which is lost in the emergence of scores of Black colleges and in the

endless procession of well-prepared Blacks taking their places
in every aspect of life in America.

Samuel Dewitt Proctor, Ph. D.

Martin Luther King Professor of Education
Department of Social and Philosophical
    Foundations of Education
Graduate School of Education
Rutgers University
New Brunswick, New Jersey

I. BLACK EDUCATION IN VIRGINIA, 1619-1861

Introduction

The history of the education of the Black race in the Virginia Colony was inexorably interwoven with the history of the church. The teaching of Blacks by church missionaries began there in 1619, when the first twenty Black indentured servants landed at Jamestown. It remained a function of the church until the consciousness of the "rights of man" gained popularity and slavery became a prominent issue. [1]

Brought to this country from the African wilds to make up the laboring class of pioneering society, the heathen slaves had to be prepared to meet the needs of the new environment. Although it was generally considered a crime to teach a slave to read and write in those states in which the holding of slaves was legal, kind masters allowed missionaries to teach their slaves those skills on a regular basis. In many instances, the masters taught their slaves personally or required members of their households to do so. Intelligent masters knew that slaves who had some understanding of the culture and language of their masters would be of far more value than ignorant ones with whom they could not communicate. Further, most of the slaveholders were religious and trusted the missionaries to teach their slaves without encouraging the overthrow of the institution of slavery. The slave masters were aware that the churches, in general, remained neutral on the slave issue and there was little danger of their missionaries becoming activists against slavery.

While the education of slaves in Virginia depended largely on the generosity of slave owners, there was little prejudice against the education of free Blacks. [2] From 1643, when there were only a small number of free Blacks in Vir-

ginia, until the beginning of the nineteenth century, when the
free Black population had reached nearly twenty thousand, apprenticeship laws were enacted that made it compulsory to
educate certain free Black children and the poor white children of the colony. [3]

The apprenticeship system, which gave rise to the
"pauper schools," was the first suggestion of compulsory
education in Virginia and was the beginning of industrial and
vocational training. The Anglican church brought the system
to America. It was an aristocratic plan of education based
on the conception that those members of society who were too
poor to pay for their education should become educated at
public expense while those who could afford to do so would
be educated in church or private schools. The system created class distinctions and was met by considerable opposition in Virginia and other states. [4]

In late 1800, due to an attempted insurrection at Richmond led by a slave named Gabriel, a restriction was placed
on the education of free Blacks and slaves for fear that they
would attempt to overthrow slavery. [5]

Michael Katz postulates that America acquired its
fundamental educational structure in the late eighteenth and
first half of the nineteenth centuries. Based on the apprenticeship system (pauper schools) that was then in effect,
bureaucracy, class bias, and racism emerged to characterize
the nation's educational system. By 1880, the shape, purpose,
and function of the American educational system became fixed
on these structural characteristics and has not changed
since. [6]

Katz argues that the basis of American education has
been the inculcation of attitudes "that reflect dominant social
and industrial values," with a bureaucratic structure. To
accomplish this there have been four alternative modes of organizing public education in America: paternalistic voluntarism, democratic localism, corporate voluntarism, and incipient bureaucracy. [7]

Paternalistic voluntarism describes one class in society that has volunteered to educate another to ensure that the
rudiments of literacy and morality are imparted. Democratic
localism refers to the control of education that rests with the
district or community. It assumes that the absolute control
of education should remain with the people themselves. Cor-

porate voluntarism indicates the educational mode through
which single institutions, primarily secondary and higher education institutions, were conducted as individual corporations
operated by self-perpetuating boards of trustees and financed
entirely through endowment or through a combination of endowment and tuition. Incipient bureaucracy signifies the mode
that centralized education and placed it on a universal basis
with free schools, which children were required to attend
through a certain age. [8]

The education of Blacks in Virginia during the antebellum period was primarily based on the paternalistic-
voluntarism mode of education. After the Civil War, all
four modes, to varying degrees, reflected the fundamental
structure of Black education in Virginia, as it did other citizens of the state.

The Colonial Era, 1619-1775

There were at least two schools of thought among the colonists concerning the education of slaves. One contended that
education would generate or intensify a longing for freedom
and that the slaves could be better controlled in ignorance.
The other school favored educating Blacks, but for diverse
reasons. Some felt it was practical to educate them, as it
was the economically feasible thing to do; others sympathized
with the plight of the slaves and believed that to educate them
was to relieve them of some of their misery; still others
were zealous missionaries who desired to convert the heathen
slaves to Christianity. [9]

The school of thought that favored education for Black
slaves prevailed and was pervasive throughout the colony until 1667, when opponents to the practice protested vehemently.
They declared that they understood the British common law
to mean that to Christianize slaves made it mandatory to
free them. Their protests were so strong that the General
Assembly of Virginia enacted a resolution in 1667 that declared that the baptizing of a person did not change his or
her status as to slavery or freedom. [10]

Even though the General Assembly of Virginia made
it clear through its enactment of 1667 that Chritianizing slaves
did not mean they were to be freed, opponents to the education of slaves continued to voice their disapproval. As a
result, in 1678 the General Assembly was moved to enact

another law on the subject.   It forbade the Quakers, who
were then at the forefront in teaching slaves and free Blacks
to read and write, from teaching slaves further until they
(the Quakers) had taken an oath of allegiance and supremacy.
This requirement was highly inconsistent with the spirit and
creed of the Quakers, so they were unable to continue teaching slaves. [11]   The matter was not resolved until 1685, when
the Bishop of London interceded and declared that the British
common law did not imply that conversions meant manumission.   The antagonists were pleased with this decision.   From
the time it was rendered, religious groups began organizing
their efforts to work together and systematically to enlighten
Blacks throughout the Virginia Colony. [12]

     Results obtained by the religious groups that partici-
pated in enlightening Blacks in the colony show that their efforts were productive.   As an example, in the early eighteenth century, reports of an increase in the number of Black
communicants came from Accomac County, Virginia, where
four or five hundred families were instructing their slaves at
home and had their children catechized on Sunday. [13]   In 1724,
an individual identified only as Lambeth published a document
that declared it was the duty of the Virginia masters and mistresses to educate their slaves and proposed that every slave
who was Christianized and brought into the church before age
fourteen should be exempted from all levies until age eighteen. [14]

     The tremendous desire for learning on the part of
Blacks and the favorable attitude of many Virginians toward
providing them with education in the first half of the eighteenth
century once again caused consternation in the colony.   Some
adversaries protested that Blacks when converted became more
saucy than pious, and due to their stubborness there could be
no close dealing with them.   Others declared that slaves were
so ignorant and disobedient that it was simply vain to teach
them to read and write.   Less cruel slaveholders rationalized
that it was just too time consuming to instruct their slaves.
This group maintained that it required more time and labor
to teach their slaves Christian principles than they had to
spare.   There were still others who confessed that they were
just too ignorant themselves to teach others. [15]

     In 1727, the Bishop of London interceded again to set-
tle the agitation in the colony over the education of Black
slaves.   On this occasion, he wrote the colonists a stinging
letter exhorting them to encourage and promote the education
of Blacks at every opportunity.   He also sent letters to the

missionary organizations directing them to give whatever assistance they could to the work of educating Blacks. [16]

Despite the opposing views on the education of Blacks in the Virginia Colony, a large number of Blacks were accorded treatment as human beings capable of mental, moral, and spiritual development. Some members were generous to the extent of providing their slaves with tutors, while still others provided them with schools. Some Blacks were also taught in classes with the children of their masters. In some cases, when Blacks experienced sufficient mental development to qualify as teachers themselves, they were called upon to teach their masters' children. [17]

The evidence for the mental development of the slaves in the Virginia Colony is found in the words of the masters themselves. When masters offered slaves for sale or advertised for their runaways, they often publicized their slaves' virtues as well as shortcomings. From what was contained in many of the advertisements of the period, it must be concluded that many colonial Virginia slaves had become enlightened and made themselves useful and skilled laborers. Some had a knowledge of the modern languages, the fundamentals of mathematics and science, and acquaintance with some of the professions. It was very common to refer to certain slaves as being smart and having mental development comparable with what is now termed an elementary-level education. Some spoke "good English," in contradistinction to others who spoke "very much broken English." In other cases, slaves were credited with speaking "proper English" or "very properly."[18]

A high percentage of slaves were brought to this country from the West Indies, where many of them had gained good educations. There they had been in contact with all European nationalities and had not been restricted in their development. It was not unusual to find a slave who spoke Spanish, French, and very good English. [19]

In addition to having had the knowledge to express themselves fluently in the modern languages, a large number of the fugitive slaves who were advertised in the Virginia Colony had learned to read and write. Many of the advertisements for fugitive slaves during the eighteenth century revealed that a high percentage of them could read and write. [20]

While the Virginia colonists debated the pros and cons

of educating slaves, free Black children were being educated at public expense under the apprenticeship system, which became generally known as the "pauper system." The first apprenticeship law in Virginia was enacted by the General Assembly of Virginia in 1643. It was based on the British law of 1601, which required the guardians of orphans to educate and instruct the children committed to their care by the church or the court "in the Christian religion and the rudiments of learning, and to provide for them necessaries according to the competence of their estates."[21] In 1691, another apprentice law was enacted, which required that free mulatto bastards be bound by the church wardens as apprentices until they became thirty years of age.[22] By the act of 1705, one year was added to the period of apprenticeship.[23] In 1727, still another apprentice law was enacted, which made it lawful for church wardens to designate as apprentices children whose parents were incapable of properly caring for and educating them in Christian principles. The law of 1727 was extended in 1748 so as to authorize guardians to apprentice dependent orphans, or neglected boys, to tradesmen, merchants, or mechanics and girls to suitable mistresses. In 1774, the apprenticeship laws were revised to shorten the apprenticeship to twenty-one years of age for males and eighteen for females.[24]

The Revolutionary War Era, 1776-1783

During the Revolutionary period, Virginia's investment in the education of some of her slaves paid great dividends, but that did not cause her to accelerate educational assistance. Although Blacks were not allowed to enroll legally in the Virginia militia as soldiers, thousands "joined up" and proved to be of great service to the land forces. Many Blacks followed the militia units as laborers, but quite a few of the more educated performed intelligence functions by acting as spies, messengers, and guides.[25] The most prominent of the Black intelligence agents of the Revolutionary War was James, a very intelligent slave who was the subject of William Armistead of New Kent County, Virginia. With the permission of his master, he served with Major General Marquis de Lafayette at Williamsburg, in 1781, where Lafayette was engaged in the fight against Benedict Arnold's forces. James was sent to Arnold's headquarters to gather information on the troop strength, battle plans, and other general matters. He performed his duty in such a manner that General Lafayette praised him highly for his action.[26]

Before the Revolutionary War was concluded, many
Blacks, both slave and free, served with great valor in the
land and sea forces. So much so did they contribute to the
war effort that many slaves were manumitted upon their return from service. Their war efforts, fortunately, extended
far beyond manumission on the part of a few. Many Americans whose consciences were stirred by the fact that the war
had been fought over the issue of liberty, and that slavery
was inconsistent with that ideal, commenced to reflect seriously
on the slave issue. Concern was demonstrated through the
formation of abolition societies, in antislavery activities of
state and federal governments, in the display of greater interest in the welfare of Blacks by the church, and in the increase of efforts by slaves for their own emancipation. [27]

The Anglican church continued to promote the charity-
school concept of education during this period. By so doing,
it obstructed the acceptance of the universal-education doctrine
that was conceived by Thomas Jefferson, which espoused the
belief that the diffusion of knowledge among all the people of
the State of Virginia, Black and white, was essential to the
preservation of freedom and happiness. To this end, Jefferson had worked to create a system that would give all inhabitants of Virginia an opportunity for at least an elementary education. All expenses connected with the plan were to be provided out of public funds. For this purpose, in 1779, he
drafted a proposal, the "Bill for the More General Diffusion
of Knowledge," which was designed to make Virginia into a
thoroughly democratic state. [28]

Unfortunately, Virginia, as well as other southern
colonies, was unprepared to accept such a democratic approach
to education. Slavery had first to be abolished and the people
freed from a feudal system before the colonists would even
begin to consider the idea. The South did not become the
democracy Jefferson dreamed of until nearly one hundred years
had elapsed.

Notwithstanding the fact that slavery lasted more than
three-fourths of a century beyond the beginning of the Revolutionary War, there can be no doubt that the beginning of the
push to eradicate slavery in America began during this period.

The National Era, 1784-1831

The history of the Black race during the National Era is

characterized by acceptance, rejection, and revolution. This
period, more than any other in history, witnessed more active involvement of religious organizations in the teaching of
religious subjects to Blacks in Virginia. With a Black population of three hundred and four thousand in 1790, which was
the largest of any southern state, Virginia was considered to
be a fertile place in which to intensify their Christianization
efforts and perhaps sabotage the institution of slavery. Among
the religious denominations were the Quakers, Methodists,
Presbyterians, Catholics, and Baptists. The Black population
was very receptive to their efforts, as they knew that any
knowledge gained would serve them well if and when they
gained freedom. [29] The leading denomination among the Blacks
of Virginia was the Baptist church. Many of the Baptist
churches admitted Blacks into membership and reached out
to them to become involved in religious services. The manner in which ministers of the Baptist church generally preached
the gospel in such a simple form and with such forceful appeal attracted Blacks. They found in the fiery Baptist messages of salvation a hope and a prospect of escape from their
earthly troubles. Moreover, emphasis placed on feelings as
a form of conversion ignited a spark in slaves who were re-
pressed in many ways. There were other factors too, such
as the solidarity that was achieved through worship by draw-
ing the slaves into union with their fellow men and women and
causing them temporarily to forget their problems. [30]

    In addition to conducting appealing religious services
for the slaves and emerging as the largest Black-populated
denomination, the Baptist church also moved ahead of other
denominations in the fight to eradicate slavery in Virginia.
In late 1789, the Baptist church launched such a tremendous
fight against slavery that there was created much dissention
in the organization. Proclaiming that "slavery is a violent
depredation of the rights of nature and inconsistent with a re-
publican government," it recommended that its members should
"make use of the local missions to extirpate this horrid evil
from the land." Thus, the Baptists, in 1789, moved to abolish
slavery in Virginia and in so doing incurred the admiration of
the lowly slaves. [31] This position, however, did not meet with
the approval of the entire Baptist organization, as many Baptists were slaveholders. Although they were somewhat in
agreement on educating their slaves on Christian principles,
they were not in favor of dispensing with their valuable services. In fact, this manifestation on the part of Virginia Baptists forbode a split in the church, which ultimately occurred
in 1844 over the slavery question.

A new stage was reached in the religion-education setting when white churches began accepting Blacks into their congregations in the last quarter of the eighteenth century. Most white Baptists were imbued with the idea of an equality of Blacks in the church, although they did not always militantly denounce slavery. Blacks were accepted on this basis, and certain among them were even allowed to preach in the white churches when they demonstrated the power of explicating the scriptures with reasonable erudition.

As a general rule, Black slaves were not allowed to have their own congregations when they were first allowed to worship in Baptist churches. They were allowed only to attend religious services at white churches at the discretion of their masters. This custom, however, stimulated the appetites of these poor, ignorant, and outcast people. When they desired to partake of religious activities beyond that authorized by their masters, they stole off to the woods, canebrakes, and remote cabins, where they conducted their own. Many are the stories told by ex-slaves of Virginia of having been caught worshipping deep in the woods and flogged severely by overseers or masters. Out of this practice of stealing away to the woods to worship emanated the "prayer meeting," which is still prevalent among Black Baptists. The patrols would be on duty all night to see that no Blacks assembled to worship without written consent from their masters. Early in the mornings, the patrols would retire from duty and sleep during the day. While they slept on Sunday mornings, quite some time before daybreak, slaves would gently steal away into the canebrakes and swamps to conduct prayer meetings in their own way. [32]

Slaves who attended white Baptist churches in the late eighteenth and early nineteenth centuries were, for the most part, extremely displeased with the conditions under which they were forced to worship and receive religious training. They were unhappy because they were in all instances separated from other worshippers by being given either special pews or balcony seatings and were constantly being fed special messages consisting of opiate passages concerning obedience, servitude, and humility by white preachers. [33] They resented the presentation of their masters as God. The greater proportion of them were eager to start churches of their own where they could worship more freely. As quickly as they were able to receive the sanction of their masters and break away from white Baptist churches and establish their own, they did. [34]

The first Black Baptist churches in Virginia were under white ministers. Gradually, however, as certain men
among the membership developed lives of great piety and became sufficiently sophisticated in ministering Baptist doctrine,
they were accorded the privilege to preach and finally to pastor. From 1776 to 1790, Black preachers were in charge of
congregations in Charles City, Petersburg, and Allen's Creek
in Lunenburg County, Virginia. [35]

The first Black Baptist church in Virginia was organized at Petersburg in 1776. Another was established at Williamsburg in 1785. In Portsmouth, a Black Baptist preacher,
Josiah Bishop, attained unusual distinction in 1795, when he
became pastor of a mixed congregation. He was held in such
esteem by his members that the church gave him the money
to purchase his freedom. Not long after he was freed, he
purchased the freedom of his wife and his eldest son. [36]

Bishop, although he was well liked by his members,
could not remain long as the pastor of a mixed church in the
slaveholding colony of Virginia. After pastoring successfully
at Portsmouth for several years, he moved to Baltimore,
Maryland, where he became a leader among the Black Baptists of that city. When his work was finished there, he
moved to New York City, where during 1810 and 1811 he
served as pastor of the Abyssinian Baptist Church. [37]

The history of the rise of the Blacks in the Baptist
sect is both interesting and strange. Interesting because it
depicts the struggle of a people who had their rise into Christianity under the most adverse circumstances, and strange because they have made their progress as a separate part of the
general Baptist family, and yet believe and practice all that
the white Baptists believe and practice.

The more Black churches were organized and missionary work among them was accelerated during this era, the
more the Blacks became aware of their servile status and
reached out for freedom from slavery. This period in history is marked by many conspiracies and revolts on the part
of slaves in Virginia, as well as other slaveholding states.
With the gaining of knowledge of life and religious freedom,
Blacks became increasingly weary of slavery and made even
greater attempts to destroy the institution.

A rare letter found in 1793 on a street at Yorktown,
Virginia, attests to the unrest that accompanied the enlighten-

ment of slaves during the early years of the nation. Written
by a slave at Richmond to another at Norfolk, Virginia, a
fellow conspirator in a plot to overthrow slavery in all of the
slaveholding states, it tells that nearly five hundred guns had
been collected, but very little gun powder was available. It
explains that a "gentleman" had promised to provide the plot-
ters with as much gunpowder as they wanted, and once the
revolution began, he would assist them in any way he could
to make it successful. It also pointed out that a fellow conspirator at Charleston, South Carolina, had informed the
sender that there were nearly six thousand men who stood by
there to assist in the revolt. [38]

Seven years later, in 1800, Gabriel Prosser, a learned
slave who was twenty-four years of age, initiated a slave revolt in Henrico County, Virginia, that changed the course of
educational history for Black slaves in Virginia. Gabriel, assisted by his brother Martin and a friend, Jack Bowler,
throughout the summer of 1800 held meetings at which they
explained how the scriptures had considerable bearing on the
Black man's existence and recruited men to overthrow their
oppressors at Richmond, Virginia. The insurrection was set
for September 1, 1800. It was planned that a large force of
slaves and free Blacks would come together at a brook near
Richmond and march on the city in three columns. The first
column was designated to seize the arsenal; the second, the
powder house; and the third, armed with muskets, knives,
and pikes, was to begin the attack. On the day the siege
was to begin, Henrico County, Virginia, experienced a severe
storm, the likes of which had not occurred there in years.
Roads were washed out, bridges carried away, and plantations
flooded. The Blacks from the city could not get to the meeting place, and those in the country could not get to the city.
In the meantime, while those stalwart individuals who were
gathered at the brook awaiting the storm to subside, a slave
who did not wish to see his master slain stole away and informed on the conspirators. [39] When the news reached Governor James Monroe, he took immediate action to alert local
authorities and call out the federal Cavalry. Through his efforts, the attempt to overthrow Richmond was summarily
thwarted. Gabriel and thirty of his slave cohorts were tried
and executed during the months of September and October for
plotting the insurrection. [40]

Until the Gabriel Prosser revolt, free Blacks were accorded the privilege of apprenticeship training under authority
of the statutes of the state of Virginia. In 1801, the General

Assembly of Virginia enacted legislation that prohibited Black
and mulatto orphans from being taught reading, writing, and
arithmetic, but restricted them to being taught trades only. [41]
Free Blacks who were eager to learn were thereafter restricted to private tutoring and instruction in Sunday Schools.

The General Assembly of Virginia had hoped that the
enactment of 1801, which placed a restriction on the education of free Blacks, would serve to preclude future revolts
in Virginia. This was not the case, as the corpses of Gabriel and his comrades had hardly turned cold when other
slave plots began to appear. It seems that Blacks were finally on the move to overthrow slavery in Virginia, and they
were determined that nothing would stop them. As they became more enlightened through missionary teachings and abolitionist information, their efforts to do something to relieve
themselves of their burdens became extended. In January
1802, at Nottoway County, Virginia, another revolt plot was
organized. Several Blacks suspected of planning the revolt
were executed. The same year, it was disclosed that another
revolt was projected in Goochland County, Virginia. Several
plots were revealed in 1808 and 1809 requiring almost continuous patrolling. During the War of 1812, there were reports of anticipated uprisings in the Tidewater area, around
Norfolk and Portsmouth, Virginia, and regiments were dis-
patched there to keep them from occurring. Following the
War of 1812, the efforts of slaves to revolt continued. In
1814 the city of Lynchburg and the county of Caroline petitioned the Governor of Virginia for troops in anticipation of
uprisings. In 1815, one George Boxley decided to attempt to
free the slaves. He made elaborate plans, but a slave woman
betrayed his plans to his master. Although Boxley escaped,
six slaves were hanged and another six were banished. In
the spring of 1816, Fredericksburg and Richmond were the
targets of investigations, confessions were wrung from slaves
concerning potential attacks on the two cities. [42]

By 1819, the state of Virginia was greatly concerned
about the many slave revolts that had taken place there during
the early National Era. Blame was placed on Black "schools"
for contributing to this unrest among slaves. Once again, the
General Assembly of Virginia enacted legislation with a view
to ending revolts. The law of 1819 provided that there should
be "no more assemblages of slaves or free Blacks, or mulattoes mixing and association with such slaves for teaching
them reading and writing. "[43] The opposition seemed to be
gripped by the thought that Blacks were being generally en-

lightened throughout the state by white teachers who advocated uprisings.

The panic of the first quarter of the nineteenth century culminated in 1831 with the insurrection of Nat Turner, an extremely literate young Black man of Southampton County, Virginia. Turner, who was twenty-four years of age, led a group of about sixty-five Blacks in a revolt at Jerusalem, Virginia, on August 12, 1831, which killed sixty-one white persons. He was captured on October 30, and within two weeks, on November 11, was executed. [44]

After Governor John Floyd reviewed the Nat Turner Insurrection case in late 1831, he concluded that northern agitators, in the form of missionaries and abolitionists, were responsible. He was certain that the lessons taught and liter-ature distributed contained venomous messages of hate against slavery, which sparked the revolt. On December 6, 1831, he addressed the General Assembly of Virginia and informed them of his strong beliefs and recommended that state laws be revised forthwith to preserve the slave population in due subordination.

Before the end of 1831, the General Assembly of Vir-ginia reacted to the Governor's plea by enacting legislation that provided a penalty for preaching or for attending religious services, an act that had it been enforced literally, would have spelled the doom of all Blacks in Virginia, free and enslaved. Fortunately, it was not adhered to in most instances, and Blacks were able to continue learning to read and write, but on an extremely restricted basis, while receiving religious instruction at Sunday Schools.

Another reactionary movement that took place during this period was the colonization scheme. On December 31, 1816, a group of so-called prominent Virginians who felt that Blacks had become too "uppity" and were "obnoxious to the laws or dangerous to the peace of society" formed an organi-zation called the American Colonization Society. The purpose of the organization was to formulate plans by which Blacks could be colonized in Africa. The idea was sanctioned by both the Governor of Virginia and the President of the United States. Both had exchanged extensive communications on the Gabriel Insurrection of 1800, among other uprisings, and promulgated the colonization concept. Among the society's organizers were Samuel Mills, a William and Mary College student; John Randolph, a senator from Virginia; and Judge Bushrade Washington, a brother of George Washington. [45]

In 1819, the United States Government appropriated
$100,000 toward the project and purchased a tract of land on
the West Coast of Africa, which it designated Liberia, for
colonization purposes. The government was then faced with
finding sufficient literate Blacks to send there to make the
colonization plan operational. The government desired to
produce in the United States a number of literate Blacks
around whom the government could be formed in Liberia. To
this end, the government established better institutions of
learning for Black youth who were to be sent to Liberia. Occasionally, Virginia planters, and other planters in slaveholding states who were interested in the colonization plan, would
free certain of their slaves and send them to eastern schools
to become educated and better prepared for higher life in their
new home in Africa. In general, Blacks were encouraged to
develop the power to work out their own salvation. It gave
an impetus to the movement on the part of Blacks for more
thorough education at the very time the South was attempting
to restrict such opportunities. A short time after the colonization plan became operational, the Society was in a dilemma.
While it told the nation that because the free Blacks were a
depraved class they could not be elevated, it also encouraged
Blacks to promote the education of those who were to be deported. It was the government's desire to raise the level of
mental development of those Blacks who were to be deported
to that which was considered necessary for whites for citizenship. [46]

Among the missionaries to Liberia was Lott Carey,
who was born a slave at Richmond in 1780. For a number
of years in his young life, he worked in a tobacco factory.
In 1807, he was converted to Christianity by missionaries,
after which he made rapid advance in education and was li-
censed a Baptist preacher. He purchased his own freedom
and that of his children (his first wife having died), organized
a missionary society, and then in 1821 went to Liberia as a
missionary. He remained there, working heroically in the
interest of the colonists, until his death in 1828. [47] The missionary society he founded is now designated the Lott Carey
Foreign Missionary Society in honor of this great minister and
teacher, who, prior to going to Liberia, conducted a school
for Blacks at the First Baptist Church of Richmond. The
church was predominantly white and pastored by a white minister, but Blacks worshipped there. It served as the focal
point for the education of many Blacks of Richmond during the
period between the Revolutionary War and the Civil War. [48]

The American Colonization Society and all that it represented met general opposition from Black people in Virginia
throughout its existence. At a meeting of a large number of
the free Blacks of Richmond, on Friday, January 24, 1817,
a resolution was unanimously adopted that appealed to the
United States Congress to desist in the colonization movement.
It was suggested that it would be far more charitable to grant
Blacks a small territory in their native country, the United
States, than to exile them to a foreign country. [49]

Revolts, or conspiracies to revolt, persisted until the
Civil War terminated in 1865. They were integral to the institution of slavery, and nothing the whites did could stop
them. Withholding of educational privileges, killings, and
colonization efforts did not deter the Black race from rebel-
ling against its oppressors. Revolution was a kind of bitter-
ness that the whites had to take with the sweetness of slavery.
As the country turned to Jeffersonian Republicanism at the beginning of the nineteenth century, many people believed that a
new day was dawning for the common person. Some Blacks,
however, were not so optimistic. They believed that they
would have to force their new day by overthrowing the institution of slavery, which many attempted to do during the National Era.

Education and Religion of Blacks, 1832-1861

From 1832 until the outbreak of the Civil War in 1861, Blacks
experienced perhaps more fear in Virginia than at any other
time during slavery. They were attacked on both the religious
and educational fronts, and the most humiliating, debilitating,
and degrading laws were passed to preclude them from partak-
ing of either religious or educational activities.

It was during this time span that many educated Blacks
emerged to lead their people in the fight for human rights and
dignity. Among the great Black leaders who emerged to fight
against the institution of slavery and its concomitant oppressive laws were William Still (1821-1902), the Underground
Railroad leader; Harriet Tubman (1826-1913), another Underground Railroad leader; Sojourner Truth (1797-1883), an orator
against slavery; Frederick Douglass (1817-1895), an abolitionist; and Alexander Crummell (1819-1898), an abolitionist minister.

After the Nat Turner Insurrection, the education of

Blacks was regarded as being positively inconsistent with the peculiar institution of slavery.   Through Virginia, and many parts of the South, attitudes toward Blacks were extremely negative.   So bad was the treatment of Blacks in Virginia that Delegate Berry of the House of Delegates declared in 1832:

> We have so far as possible closed every possible avenue by which light may enter their (the slaves) minds.   If we could extinguish the capacity to see the light, our work would be completed; they then would be on the level with the beasts of the field and we should be safe!   I am not certain that we would not do it if we could find the process and that on the plea of necessity. [50]

Suffering under the law that brought to an end the education of all Blacks, a group of well-to-do free Blacks of Fredericksburg, Virginia, petitioned the General Assembly in 1838 for permission to conduct a school, because of the great expense involved in sending their children North.   One of their significant contentions was:

> ... Knowledge now has been so diffused that persons who are uneducated are cut off from the ordinary means of self advancement and find the greatest difficulty in finding an honest livelihood by consequence of these conditions and prohibitionary statutes of Virginia.... [51]

The request was denied, and to add insult to injury the problem was made more difficult by passage of a bill that year making it illegal for free Blacks to return to Virginia after going North to be educated.

Notwithstanding the law and public opinion, some white persons in Virginia were deeply interested in Blacks and persisted in teaching them to read and write.   Traveling in Richmond in 1852, Frederick Law Olmsted was told by a well-informed capitalist and slaveholder that Blacks were receiving much better educational privileges than ever before.   Olmsted was surprised to learn that throughout the state, despite laws to the contrary, meetings were being held in which Blacks participated and received religious instruction as well as instruction in reading, writing, and arithmetic. [52]

In 1854, in Norfolk, a white woman, a Mrs. Douglas,

was arrested by town officials for running a school for Blacks, which had been in operation for over three years.   It was evident that the school had not been run clandestinely, but the general opposition to the education of Blacks then had been so weak that the authorities had not bothered to close the school earlier.   When Mrs. Douglas was brought before the court for violating the laws of the state of Virginia, her case was dismissed when she promised solemnly not to teach Black children to read and write again. [53]

Throughout this extremely oppressive period, many thousands of Virginia Blacks were impelled to learn to read and write.   While many were allowed to participate in the learning process by kind masters, many others learned to read and write on their own initiative.   Their efforts to educate themselves enabled them to obtain considerable knowledge and motivated them to continue to pursue education through any means possible.

Despite the antiworship laws prevalent in Virginia from 1831 to 1861, many Black Baptist churches were organized. The African Baptist Church of Richmond was founded in 1841 with nearly seven hundred members; another Black Baptist church was founded at Norfolk in 1845 with five hundred and ninety members; and three Black Baptist churches were founded at Petersburg in 1848 with a composite total of twenty-five hundred members. [54]

These churches, among many others scattered throughout Virginia that were pastored by white ministers, were the main places of refuge for Blacks who were not privileged to meet alone.   Instruction was confined to the catechism and memorization of hymns and special passages of the Bible under direct supervision of the pastor and selected deacons who were keenly aware of the Virginia laws.

From 1832 to 1862, the Black minister had to divide his attention so as to take care of all the varying interests of his persecuted brothers and sisters.   During the long years, Black Baptist ministers were compelled to support themselves by working somewhere, but often had to devote much of their time to problems of education, abolition, colonization, and the Underground Railroad.   One of the most interesting men of the type was Leonard A. Grimes, a Baptist minister who was born at Leesburg, Virginia, in 1815.   Although he was a free Black, he was subjected to all the disabilities that his race had to endure in the South short of actual slavery.   In his

youth, he spent much of his time learning the butcher's trade
and working at an apothecary's establishment in Washington,
D. C. Accompanying his employer on a trip throughout the
South, he witnessed slavery in its worst form and made a
decision to make every effort to destroy the evil. Around
1840, he began working with the Underground Railroad, in
connection with which he rendered valuable service through
assisting many slaves to escape slavery. His civil-rights
"antics" resulted in a two-year prison sentence at Richmond,
Virginia. Upon his release, he continued to fight for human
rights until his death in 1873. [55]

As the Black churches increased in number and membership in the state of Virginia, Blacks became more fervent
in their zeal for religion and education. Blacks almost worshipped the Bible, and their eagerness to read it was their
greatest incentive to learn. Therefore, many of them resorted to attending churches in the hope that they would be
able to learn to read. Out of this practice, Blacks developed
an immense thirst for knowledge, which they were to carry
with them out of slavery.

Summary

The history of the education of Blacks in Virginia prior to
1861 is divided into distinct periods. The first period ex-
tends from 1619, when slavery was introduced in America at
Jamestown, to 1831, when Nat Turner attempted to overthrow
the institution. This period witnessed the majority of Virginians answering affirmatively the question of whether or
not it was prudent to educate their slaves. Then followed
the second period, when Nat Turner's Insurrection changed
the entire approach to Black Education. White Virginians
reached the conclusion that it was impossible to cultivate the
minds of Blacks without arousing them to assert themselves
to revolt. Virginia authorities enacted laws that suppressed
instruction beyond that of memory training on the Bible. [56]

The contrast of conditions between the two periods is
striking. From 1619 through 1831, most slaves who learned
to read and write were considered extremely valuable. After
1831, those who were able to read and write were considered
unfit for service in Virginia and were branded as objects of
suspicion. Moreover, when within a generation or so, Blacks
began to retrograde because they had been deprived of every
elevating influence, the white Virginian resorted to asserting

that to enlighten Blacks would prove futile on account of their mental inferiority. [57]

Dark as the future of the Blacks in Virginia seemed during the thirty years preceding the Civil War, all hope was not yet gone. Certain white men and women there made it possible for a percentage of them to learn in spite of opposition. Preachers, on finding out that they could not convey Christian truth to undeveloped minds, in many instances taught the Black people as they did before the Nat Turner Insurrection. Blacks themselves, regarding learning as a forbidden fruit that they desired so much to eat, stole away to secret places to quench their insatiable desire for learning.

Although there were few literate Blacks when the Civil War began, there were a considerable number who had been exposed to some education and had the desire to learn. It is not surprising then that so many Blacks in Virginia became involved in learning programs in 1861 as they became available.

II. BLACK EDUCATION DURING THE CIVIL WAR, 1861-1865

Introduction

Christianized to have faith in Almighty God and to rely on omnipotent wisdom, Blacks believed unfalteringly that the day would come when the yoke of slavery would be removed from their heads. Those who were able to read the many liberation messages that filtered down to them were keenly aware that a high condition of unrest pervaded the nation in early 1861, but did not conceive that it would soon erupt into a great civil war. After two hundred and forty-two years of living in the darkness of appalling slavery, a dawn of bright freedom was finally on the horizon for millions of slaves.

The Dawn

Blacks experienced the dawn when Abraham Lincoln became President on January 1, 1861. Several months thereafter, on April 12, 1861, all of the abolition efforts of such stalwarts as Nat Turner, Frederick Douglass, John Brown, among countless others, culminated in the collision of Union and Confederate forces at Fort Sumter, South Carolina, a federal garrison. This confrontation marked the official beginning of the Civil War, fought over the issue of slavery, which lasted until August 1865.

Late in 1861, as the Civil War progressed and spread to Virginia, slaves poured forth from the Virginia plantations by the thousands and sought refuge in the federal lines. The majority of them ventured to Fortress Monroe, Virginia, a federal garrison under command of General Benjamin Butler. In the absence of specific federal guidelines as to what should be done under such circumstances, General Butler exercised his discretion and declared the Blacks "contraband of war." He then put them to work with his military force. [1]

The Blacks who came straggling into the Union lines were hungry, ragged, ignorant, confused by their wretched plight, and begging for protection. The first necessities were food, shelter, clothing, and in some cases immediate medical attention. They were escaped slaves, and since it had been decided they were contrabands, consideration had to be given to provide them with permanent relief. Something had to be done to prepare them to take care of their own needs and make an honest living in the future. In the new life of independence they were entering, they had everything to learn. The sorry, paltry creatures had to be taught just about in the same manner as their forebears were when they arrived at Jamestown in 1619. They had to be taught to behave in their new world; to work and do their work well; to use good English and to play the part of responsible men.

The federal government was keenly aware that these needs were to be met for the contrabands, but moved slowly in developing policy to provide for them. While the government dragged its feet, private persons, Black and white, northerner and southerner, and certain religious and philanthropic organizations undertook the supreme task of helping these pitiful people to become settled in freedom. [2]

Benevolent Activities

Teachers for the contrabands were forthcoming immediately after their plight became known throughout the nation in mid-1861. Hundreds of them came forth to volunteer their services: cultivated, high-minded, bent on accomplishing this big undertaking with a determination not unlike that of Francis Xavier, Henry Martyn, and Adoniram Hudson. And like these messengers to the Orient, they too, made their errand one of religious purpose. They did not see it as possible to make these fugitive slaves into decent, law-abiding, industrious people without giving them a new character, a changed life. They were of the opinion that the fugitives had to be led into an intelligent religion that should govern the whole round of their conduct. This required bringing them to the Bible, which meant that all of them were to be taught to read at the onset.[3]

The first agency to reach out to extend educational assistance to the contrabands was the American Missionary Association. Through the interest manifested by its treasurer, Lewis Tappan, it became involved in educating Blacks at Fortress Monroe on September 5, 1861, on a paternalistic-voluntarism basis when it opened a Sunday School in the home of

ex-President Tyler. Two days later, the first day school
was opened under control of the association at Hampton with
a free Black woman, Mary S. Peake, as the teacher.[4] In
1862, the field was enlarged to include Newport News, Virginia, and Washington, D. C.; in 1865, the Association had
three hundred and fifty-three persons employed in church and
school work among Blacks throughout the South.[5] In the state
of Virginia, there were more than three thousand Blacks attending school with fifty-two teachers, five of whom were
Black. The American Missionary Association paid the teachers, while the federal government granted them subsistence.[6]

    The American Missionary Association was from the
start nonsectarian. In June 1865, it consisted of the Congre-
gational, the Free Will Baptist, the Wesleyan Methodist, and
the Reformed Dutch church organizations. It had been established in 1846 as a protest against the "comparative silence
of other missionaries with regard to slavery. "[7]

    The American Baptist Home Mission Society, founded
at New York City in 1832, also became actively involved in
educational work among former slaves in Virginia in 1862 on
a paternalistic-voluntarism basis. A representative of the
organization went to Fortress Monroe on January 30, 1862,
to conduct a study of the specific needs of the refugees. As
a result of that study, the society organized the "Freedmen's
Committee" to work among the contrabands. The committee
was given the responsibility for "raising funds and sending
out and recommending suitable persons for assistants in the
South. "[8] By 1864, the society was deeply engaged in teaching
freed slaves throughout Virginia.

    The methods of the American Baptist Home Mission
Society contemplated three things: General Missionary work
in winning more Blacks to Christ and gathering them into
churches; secular education to enable Blacks to learn to read
and write; and the education of Black ministers through special classes with the objective of getting them to go back
among their people and lead them out of ignorance and into
the church. The society held that the freed slaves looked up
to those among them who were preachers. Therefore, the
Black preachers were conceived as leaders and as such, according to the American Baptist Home Mission Society's thinking, should be educated to lead their own people. It was
thought that if it concentrated solely on educating the Black
youth of Virginia, as well as other southern states, eventually
they would look down on the lowly, ignorant Black preachers

from their higher intellectual plane.   The preachers would
thence lose their leadership influence and the educated Black
youth would drift into immorality and infidelity.   To accomplish this, the society concentrated on establishing formally
structured institutions of higher learning for Black preachers. [9]

   To this end, the Society's first appointment was in
April 1865 at Richmond, where Dr. J. G. Binney, at one
time President of Columbian College, Washington, D. C. , began instructing Black men, young and aging, preparing for
the ministry. [10]   This project marked the official beginning
of the institution now known as Virginia Union University,
which had grown through the years to become a major source
of Black ministers in the nation.

The Black Church and Education During the Civil War

The outbreak of the Civil War was also an outbreak in the
Black Baptist church.   Encouraged by the affliction of the
Civil War to free them, many of the Black Baptists of Virginia hoped that the state to which they had given of their
blood, sweat, and tears would repent of its sins and grant
them the privilege of living in honor and decency.   As they
poured forth from slavery, even as contrabands as early as
1861, Blacks commenced organizing new Baptist churches
and consolidating their efforts to influence Virginia to regard
them as human beings.   The pressure having been removed
from being slaves, groups of Blacks who had long awaited
religious freedom found ample opportunity for exercising it
in the organization of numerous Black Baptist churches over
the entire state.   This was not abruptly effected in all cases,
as the Blacks were very poor and had to pool their meager
resources for long periods to get their physical plants
started. [11]

   Black Baptist churches throughout Virginia placed great
emphasis on individual improvement.   They stressed that it
was the duty of the church to educate the masses, elevate the
laity, and Christianize the heathen. [12]   As early as 1861, at
the beginning of the Black Baptist church buildup effort, inter-
denominational interaction took place frequently between whites
and Blacks to exchange ideas concerning how the aim of educating Blacks could best be accomplished.

   The impetus on the part of Black Baptist churches
toward education was based on the desire of the leaders to

refute the belief generally held that Blacks were incapable of the mental development known to whites. Thus, education of the Black race was both a test and challenge to Black ministers. They were determined to show the world that the Black race, if given the proper opportunity, could hold its own in the intellectual world and thereby prove that the Black race was not inferior to other people. They were determined to prove that Blacks could master subjects such as grammar, language, and Latin, Greek, and Hebrew literature. Questions to be resolved by the church were: Are Black Americans capable of understanding the important things of life as exposited by mathematicians, philosophers, and scientists? Can they learn to think? Of course, there were isolated instances where Black Virginians had demonstrated some proficiency in these fields during the period, but their achievements were mostly accounted for by their racial connection with the white race, or with some Arabic stock of Africa, known to be caucasian rather than Negroid. [13]

The main reason that the Black minister emphasized education during this period is because it was realized that the church needed it in advancing its work.

With the many denominational groups working together to promote religious education during the Civil War, the Black Baptist churches soon had a large number of men equipped to extend their work. Gradually, the emphasis shifted from teaching Blacks the religious ideas and practices of the culture to teaching them the intrinsic value of education.

Blacks as Military Personnel

At the beginning of 1863, immediately after the Emancipation Proclamation, Blacks were allowed to enlist in the United States Army, to which there was an immediate and heavy response. Before the end of 1863, there were 100,000 former slaves in the military service, about half of whom were assigned as combatants. By the close of the war, the total number of Black troops had risen to 186,000.

Military life had considerable influence on the men who enlisted, and they in turn had similar influence on those they came in contact with upon the termination of their enlistments. Taken into the military service without settled abodes or regular occupation, they were exposed to the orderly habits and rigid discipline of a soldier's life, which was a very effective school for providing them with values for future living. Of the values imparted to the Black soldiers, education was perhaps the one they were most amenable to.

The esteem in which education was held by Black soldiers can be judged best by the time they expended and efforts they made to educate themselves and to establish a system of education for others of their race. Doubtless, many persons believed that the Black soldier was so preoccupied with his recent release from slavery that he was contented with his lot, that his patriotism was confined solely to the battlefield simply to ensure his freedom. Such a supposition was far from the truth. Black soldiers in the Civil War had a tremendous race pride, and the idea that ignorance was the cause of their oppression gave zest to their desire to become educated. [14]

When the Black soldiers found a large number of northern educators following the United States Army, establishing schools wherever they could in village, city, and camp, and that the education was free to all, there was awakened in the Black soldier's breast an ambition, not only to obtain knowledge, but to contribute part of his small earnings in aid of educational institutions. This was done on a very liberal basis, both during and subsequent to the war. [15]

Unlettered themselves, they became more deeply impressed daily, through their military associations and by contact with things that required knowledge, with the necessity of becoming educated. Each soldier felt that but for his illiteracy he might be a sergeant, company clerk, or quartermaster; not a few felt that, if educated, they might be lieutenants and captains. This was not an unusual conclusion for a brave soldier to arrive at, when men no braver than himself were being promoted for bravery. [16]

Having traveled extensively and observed many Black units, Joseph Wilson, a Black Captain in the Civil War said:

> ... there was one of three things the Black soldier could be generally found during at leisure: discussing religion, cleaning his equipment, or trying to read. His zeal frequently led him to neglect to eat for the latter. Every camp had a teacher, in fact every company had someone to instruct the soldiers in reading, if nothing more. Since the war I have known of more than one who has taken up the pro-

fession of preaching and law making, whose first letter was earned in camp; and not a few have entered college. [17]

In an article titled "The Schoolmaster in the Army," published in Fortune magazine several years after the Civil War, Lieutenant James Trotter, a Civil War veteran and later a Registrar of Deeds at Washington, D.C., said that many Black soldiers secured an education in the army and gained, in some cases, great proficiency. [18]

The Black soldier was not only patriotic in the highest sense but was a keen observer of both the advantages and opportunities of his race. He recognized that the general education of the members of the Union Army in comparison with the educational level of those who composed the Confederate Army, gave them great advantage over the enemy. The ingenuity of the Yankee he attributed to his education, and he readily decided he lacked only the Yankee's education to be his equal in genius. The incentive given by the Yankee was highly exemplary to the Black soldier. It aroused his latent hope to be something more than a free man; if not that, his children might rise from the cotton field to the higher walks of life. The Black soldiers went forth from the Civil War to their various communities with a strong disposition to helping their fellow freedmen to become educated.

Bureau of Refugees, Freedmen, and Abandoned Lands

Before the close of the Civil War, on March 3, 1865, Congress acquiesced to the pleas of concerned citizens who pushed for action in behalf of the fugitives, and established the Freedmen's Bureau in the War Department. The agency was assigned responsibility for looking after the housing, educational, health, and labor interests of the emancipated Blacks throughout the South. Although this action was taken years later than it should have been, the organization proved to be a very successful venture. During the years of its existence, from 1865 to 1871, it not only promoted the value of education to Blacks but established over four thousand schools throughout the South, from the elementary grades through college. Nearly a quarter of a million ex-slaves received varying amounts of education through the Bureau's efforts. [19]

Summary

Having been trained in slavery to depend wholly upon the white race for leadership, encouragement, and support, Black refugees from slavery welcomed and cooperated with the northern missionaries who went to Fortress Monroe, Virginia, to teach them. Stimulated to become self-sustaining, Blacks demonstrated a great eagerness to learn. Many were the tales of ambition and aptitude for learning, as well as docility and good behavior, sent home by the teachers from the North.

The Black Baptists of Virginia came to the forefront during the Civil War and, after realizing that the state of Virginia was not acting to assist the war refugees to become socialized, joined with other denominational groups to assist their Black brothers and sisters to become adjusted to their new life. Initially, the specific objective of the church was to Christianize the refugees, but as years passed and the war came to an end, the Black Baptist church concentrated on educating Blacks for its intrinsic value.

Black soldiers who served in the Civil War took advantage of every opportunity to obtain an education. They were eager to learn and demonstrated a high aptitude for doing so. Their ambitions were to elevate themselves and to return to their communities and assist in elevating their fellow freedmen so that they could rise from the lowest level of depravity and ignorance to higher levels of decency and intelligence.

The Freedmen's Bureau represented the main national effort to assist the ex-slaves to become adjusted to their new status in the South. As a temporary agency, its appropriations were renewed year to year, until it went out of operation.

At the conclusion of the Civil War, Black freedmen in Virginia had been exposed to elementary education on a rather large scale, having been rendered educational assistance by missionary and benevolent groups and in the military service by kind commissioned and noncommissioned officers.

Despite having been educated through what Michael Katz described as the paternalistic-voluntarism mode of education, Blacks profited greatly from the educational experience. The stage was now set for what was to become a major effort to develop on this educational base and give it momentum to advance the higher education of Black Virginians in the future.

III. THE BLACK EXPERIENCE IN VIRGINIA DURING
      RECONSTRUCTION, 1865-1877

Introduction

Analysis of the events of the immediate post-Civil War period, commonly referred to as Reconstruction, is of great im-
port to this study, as it had a profound impact on the social-
ization of the Black race. Lessons learned as a result of
that historical episode served to awaken newly freed Blacks
to the harsh reality of what they could expect to confront educationally, politically, and socially in the future. They
learned that even though they were legally freed from slavery,
they were not yet freed socially. They were not yet free to
become accepted as full-fledged members of the society in
which they existed. They also learned that to gain acceptance
into the mainstream of that society would entail initiating and
promulgating much of the action on their own behalf.

    The decision by Black Baptists of Virginia to establish
and support their own secondary schools, in the last quarter
of the nineteenth century, is highly attributable to the Black
experience in regard to education during Reconstruction.

    It all started when Andrew Johnson became President
of the United States on April 15, 1865, after the sudden death
of Abraham Lincoln on April 14, 1865. [1] Johnson favored
white home rule for the ex-Confederate states, whereas certain "radical" Republicans in Congress, led by Senator Charles
Sumner of Massachusetts and Representative Thaddeus Stevens
of Pennsylvania were of the opinion that to grant such a privilege to the southern states would nullify gains made during the
Civil War and thus relegate Blacks once again to slave status. [2]

    Less than two months after becoming President, John-
son, on May 29, 1865, issued a proclamation of amnesty to

the ex-Confederate states.   It required an oath of allegiance
of all who sought pardon and a "restoration of all rights of
property, except as to slaves. "[3] He continued thereafter to
issue proclamations of relief until Congress, in December
1865, became outraged and decided to take charge of the Reconstruction.   Thinking that President Johnson was showing
too much favoritism to the "unrestored" states, Congress
passed a resolution on that date to create the Joint Committee on Reconstruction to inquire into the condition of the
southern states and make recommendations on the manner in
which Reconstruction should proceed. [4]

On February 3, 1866, the Joint Committee on Reconstruction called seven Black Virginians from the Tidewater
area to testify on living conditions there.   One witness, Dr.
Daniel Norton, a practicing physician from Yorktown, was
asked by a committee member what would happen if the federal troops and Freedmen's Bureau were removed.   He replied succinctly: "I do not think the colored people would be
safe.   They would be in danger of being hunted and killed. "[5]

The remaining Black witnesses gave similar testimony
throughout the inquiry.   The Reverend William Thornton, a
former slave from Hampton, told of a Black woodcutter who
inadvertently cut down the tree of a white neighbor and was
killed deliberately by the neighbor for the error.

Madison Newby of Surry County told the committee
that Blacks were being abused there just as much as they had
been before the war.   He further revealed that "they patrol
our houses just as formerly.... A party of twelve or fifteen
men go around at night searching the houses of colored people, turning them out and beating them. "[6]   When asked if
Blacks wanted schooling, Newby replied, "Generally ... but
down in my neighborhood they are afraid to be caught with a
book. "[7]   He explained that there were no Black schools in
Surry County, and the white people would kill anyone who
went there to establish one. [8]

Edmund Parsons of Williamsburg, a former slave, told
committee members that freedmen were anxious to become
educated but were fearful of whites and dared not incur their
wrath. [9]

Richard R. Hill of Hampton was asked to tell whether
the Black people there were anxious to go to school.   He
answered:

Yes sir; they are anxious to go to school; we have
schools there every day that are very well filled;
and we have night schools that are very well attended, both by children and aged people; they mani-
fest a great desire for education. [10]

Based on the testimony received from the seven Tidewater witnesses, among others from the former southern
slaveholding states, Congress voted in March 1866 to seat
no representatives from an ex-Confederate state until it had
declared the state entitled to representation based on its behavior. As a follow-up to that legislation, Congress enacted
the first Civil Rights Law, which declared the freedmen to
be citizens and specifically endowed them the civil rights ad-
hering to citizens, including the right to possess real and
personal property. [11]

Having found that the southern whites possessed a
strong "vindictive and malicious hatred" of freedmen, the
Joint Committee on Reconstruction also proposed the Fourteenth Amendment to the Constitution. It defined citizenship
for blacks in clear, precise terms and reversed the traditional federal-state relationship by providing for the interven-
tion of the federal government in cases where state governments were accused of violating the constitutional rights of
the individual. The amendment was approved in June 1866. [12]

After meticulously reviewing the detailed report from
the Joint Committee on Reconstruction, Congress, once again,
in March 1867, enacted Reconstruction legislation, the essential feature of which was that ten of the southern states were
to hold constitutional conventions, the delegates to which were
to be elected by "male citizens ... of whatever race, color,
or previous condition. "[13] To enforce this enactment, the
United States Army was given responsibility for registering
all voters and supervising the polls. It seemed to the Black
people that the federal government was standing behind them
one hundred percent, an illusion that they, in time, were to
learn was not true.

The Reconstruction Act of 1867 imposed on the South a
regime that was far more difficult for it to bear than the de-
feat it suffered in the Civil War. The greater majority of
southerners were disfranchised; Blacks and their allies--loyal
southern whites and whites from the North who apparently had
come south to stay--were to enjoy the ballot for the first time.
From the southern point of view, power was being placed in

the hands of those who were least qualified to control their destiny. [14]

The constitutional conventions called in pursuance of the Reconstruction Act all contained Black members, a majority of whom were Republicans. With few exceptions, they were educated men with prior records of service in the Armed Forces. Their main concerns were relief, education, and suffrage. They lost no time in making their objectives known to their fellow members once they were elected to office. [15]

As Black suffrage became a reality in Virginia, as elsewhere in the South, efforts to intimidate Blacks intensified. The entire Reconstruction Era reeked with hostility toward Blacks on the part of a large number of whites who resisted legal and political equality for the freed slaves. Interpreting the liberal Reconstruction Constitutions and the federal Civil Rights Law as allowing mixed schools and an open door to inns, hotels, and public places of amusement, Blacks endeavored to participate in these opportunities. The whites as a majority bitterly opposed any such democratization of their institutions.

Almost before the public schools could be established, Virginians, who had never been enthusiastic about education at public expense, began to oppose the system. A few interpreted the federal Civil Rights Law to mean coeducation of the races. They believed it was better to have no education at all than to have the two races commingled. [16] Poor and ignorant whites found the very thought of civil rights for ex-slaves so intolerable that they banded together to spread terror and dismay among Black Virginians. With the assistance of oppressive groups, such as the Ku Klux Klan, hate mongers continually perpetrated violence against Blacks. Such was the Blacks' plight in Virginia as they went forth from slavery and confronted their new-found "freedom" in an atmosphere of extreme hostility.

The Freedmen's Bureau in Reconstruction

The Freedmen's Bureau, which had been established in 1865 for one year, was granted legislative authority by Congress in 1866 to remain in existence for the discharge of its educational responsibility to freedmen until 1870. Nevertheless, due to the magnitude of its operation, it was to remain in existence until 1871.

The Bureau was created to aid refugees and freed slaves by furnishing supplies and medical services, supervising labor contracts between freedmen and their employers, establishing schools, and managing confiscated or abandoned lands. Its greatest success was in education, particularly in the inculcation of free elementary education among all classes in the South. It established or supervised schools of all kinds: day or night, Sunday, and industrial schools, as well as colleges. It cooperated closely with philanthropic and religious agencies in the mainstream of many educational institutions for freedmen. Howard University, which was named after the supervisor of the Freedmen's Bureau, General O. O. Howard of Maine; Richmond Institute (now Virginia Union University); Atlanta University; Fisk University; and Hampton Institute all received Bureau assistance throughout the life of the Bureau. By 1871, when the Freedmen's Bureau ceased operating, there were approximately a quarter of a million Blacks in forty-three hundred schools throughout the Southland; the Bureau had spent more than five million dollars on its educational program. [17] This vast program incurred the anger of many southerners, who were determined to keep the white race superior and felt that to educate Blacks was to give them a feeling of superiority.

To demonstrate opposition to Black education in Virginia, the Ku Klux Klan often burned or razed schools. White teachers from the North were ostracized and occasionally run out of the community. In countless other ways, Virginia Blacks were discouraged from seeking education. In the short time since Emancipation, a pattern had already started to emerge. It indicated unequivocally that white Virginians were strongly resentful of outsiders rendering educational assistance to Blacks, and yet they were reluctant to make any effort to ameliorate conditions under which Blacks lived. [18] Blacks became so disheartened by the total experience that they decided among themselves that at the opportune time they would act to remedy the situation.

When the Freedmen's Bureau stopped operating, the work of Black education in Virginia passed into the control of the philanthropic and denominational societies that had cooperated with it over the five years of its life. [19]

Many of the schools in Virginia that had been conducted by the Freedmen's Bureau were closed due to their inability to secure financial support. Some, after a few years, were taken over by the Superintendent of Common Schools, H. R.

Ruffner, and maintained by public taxation. This was the
beginning of the incipient-bureaucracy mode of education in
Virginia, as defined by Katz. The others continued under
the supervision and support of the denominational agencies
that had fostered them in conjunction with the Bureau. The
number of small elementary schools increased, and relatively
few became secondary and higher institutions. [20] The die appeared to be cast. It appeared that if Virginia Blacks were
to obtain secondary schools to assist them in bridging the
gap between elementary and higher education, they would have
to address the matter themselves.

The Black Baptist Church in Reconstruction

The Black Baptist church expanded rapidly in Virginia during
Reconstruction. Black Baptist churches sprang up overnight
in practically every community throughout the length and
breadth of the state. Within a very short period after the
Civil War the Baptists became the leading Black denominational group there. Growth was so phenomenal that fifteen
of the more aggressive Black leaders decided among themselves in early 1867 that it would be feasible to organize a
Black Baptist Convention for the purpose of forming a larger
circle of acquaintances in the service of the Lord, better
understanding policy, gathering statistics, and performing
educational, missionary, and publication work. [21]

Acting to discharge their aim, the group met at the
Zion Baptist Church in Portsmouth on May 9, 1867, and organized the Virginia Baptist State Convention. A letter bearing the date 1871 sets the specific purpose of the organization
as follows:

> Our sole objective is a diffusion of the Gospel of
> Christ in the interest of his Kingdom, by sending
> out missionaries, planting and training Churches,
> and assisting feeble Baptist Churches in the support
> of their pastors throughout the State of Virginia as
> far lieth within the ability of this convention. [22]

To carry out its evangelical work in Virginia and missionary work abroad, the convention designated four boards:
the State Board, Foreign Mission Board, Bible and Publication Board, and the Education Board.

The fifteen members who formed the Virginia Baptist

State Convention were very alert men and women. Although all of them were not highly educated, they were aware of the importance of education to the uplift of the race. They were also aware of the unenlightened mentality of the majority of their sisters and brothers, who were several years removed from slavery. They knew too that there were more than four million human beings who were scarcely able to speak an intelligible dialect even to themselves. They were cognizant that this jabbering horde turned to the church for enlightenment, and it was the church's responsibility to be responsive to their needs. Moreover, they were knowledgeable that within their own state little or no action had been taken on the part of the state officials to provide for the education of Blacks. Further, they were eternally grateful to the Freedmen's Bureau and the philanthropic and denominational groups for the educational assistance in their behalf, but were certain that the surface had hardly been scratched. Illiteracy among their people was still extremely high and they felt it was incumbent on them to form a strong denominational organization that could do something about the matter. [23]

Regardless of the excellent leadership provided through the dynamic Virginia Baptist State Convention at its onset, the Black Baptist church experienced serious difficulties during Reconstruction as it went through the throes of attempting to resolve what its functions and ideals should be. This very question almost tore the church asunder and all but split it into conservative and progressive groups. The conservative element in control, which consisted mostly of ex-slaves who were contented with rejoicing in freedom by singing the songs of their fathers and offering vociferous praise and stentorian thanks to the Lord, became so dogmatic in its treatment of the rising progressive minority that the church for a number of years lost ground among the youth. The progressive element, which consisted of young people who had been exposed to some education by missionaries from the North, was anxious to move ahead. The progressives did not regard religion as a panacea for the ills of the race. Along with religion they insisted that education should go as its handmaiden, inasmuch as there can be little revelation of God where there is arrested mental development. [24] Despite the differences between factions within the Black Baptist church during Reconstruction, it managed to forge ahead while serving as a prime factor in the general uplift of the Black race. It was instrumental in developing a social atmosphere that was highly attractive to the Black race and brought about a spirit of belongingness unlike that which the race had experienced pre-

viously.   Attached to the church was the Sunday School, to
which young Blacks went without fear and where they eagerly
studied the Bible, learned the alphabet, and learned to read
and spell. Many of the Blacks who attended Sunday Schools
often learned more on a single Sunday than the average student acquired during the entire week.   In these Sunday Schools,
not a few Blacks laid the foundation for the more liberal education that they thereafter were to obtain in schools established by their denomination and other religious and philanthropic organizations working in their behalf. [25]

     Blazing the trail with leadership in Virginia during
Reconstruction were such Black preachers of power as Reverend James H. Holmes, for years the pastor of the First
Baptist Church of Richmond; Dr. Richard Wells, the pastor
of the Ebenezer Baptist Church in the same city; Dr. Anthony
Binga, a churchman of scholarly bearing, who wrote important dissertations on theology while pastoring the leading Baptist church in Manchester, Virginia; and Dr. William H.
Stokes, a worker of much influence in Richmond, for years
a strong advocate of Black education and champion for the
rights of the Black people. [26]

The Black Educational Experience

No mass movement in the history of this country had been
more in the American tradition than the urge that drove
Blacks toward education during the Reconstruction period.
At no time or place in America has there been exemplified
so pathetic a faith in education as the lever of racial progress.   Inspired by the great educational crusade that was
carried on by northern white missionaries who worked in conjunction with the Freedmen's Bureau, Blacks throughout the
South continued to demonstrate a great zeal for learning.
They were highly encouraged because the men and women
(or "school marms," as they were called) had faith in their
intellectual capacity and worked with them with a deep sense
of commitment. [27]

     The atmosphere in which the northern missionaries
and the Freedmen's Bureau worked to educate the Black race
was filled with adversity.   The southern fear that northern
teachers would plant the doctrine of social equality in the
minds of Blacks was basic.   In communities where Freedmen's schools were located, these teachers were rejected by
many white community members.   This is perhaps best illus-

trated by a letter written by James C. Southall of the Charlottesville Chronicle of Virginia directed to a northern teacher
of that city. Southall frankly stated the case for the many
southern people who shared his sentiments. On February 12,
1867, he wrote Anna Gardner:

> The impression among the white residents of Char-
> lottesville is that your instruction of the colored
> people who attend your school contemplates some-
> thing more than the communication of the ordinary
> knowledge implied in teaching them to read, write,
> cipher, etc. The idea prevails that you instruct
> them in politics and sociology; that you come among
> us not merely as an ordinary school teacher but as
> a political missionary; that you communicate to the
> colored people ideas of social equality with whites.[28]

Community pressure was also brought to bear upon
pupils who attended Freedmen's Schools. Peter Wookfolk,
who was a slave at Richmond prior to the city's surrender,
experienced this pressure while teaching there. On April 22,
1865, he wrote that landlords were seeking to prevent Black
parents from sending their children to school by threatening
to put them out of their houses. [29]

Antagonistic actions were widespread in Virginia.
Neither the teachers nor the pupils were safe at schools.
Marauding bands frequently attacked Freedmen's schools and
assaulted both teachers and pupils. Many of these incidents
were mischievous pranks, but most were overt expressions
of an intense resentment of any action taken to educate Blacks.
Such practices combined to keep the Freedmen's school movement unstable and the pupils and teachers insecure. They
were to set a pattern that would prevail for almost one hundred years: where official rejection of Black rights was apparent, violence against Black rights movements was open. [30]

Congressional Reconstruction made it possible for the
Black race to participate in reconstructing civil government
in the ex-Confederate states. Blacks sat in legislatures and
assisted in enacting laws that have won both the praise and
condemnation of bitter partisans. It was in South Carolina
that they wielded the greatest influence. In the first legislature, there were eighty-seven Blacks and forty whites. Nevertheless, from the onset the whites controlled the state senate,
and in 1874 the lower house as well. [31]

Very few Blacks held office in the government of Virginia during Reconstruction. Twenty-seven sat in the first legislature, and others served in minor posts. So far as the exercise of influence is concerned, Blacks were never powerful enough there to determine any policy of the government except on those occasions where they held the balance between militant factions. [32]

Two major problems preoccupied Black legislators: education and civil rights. Knowing that federal aid was essential to provide sound school systems for the South, they proposed federal land grants to provide funds for schools, but their arguments fell on deaf ears. [33] They were, however, along with the carpetbaggers and scalawags who served alongside them, instrumental in instituting systems of free public education for all children. [34]

Although several southern states established free public schools during 1868 and 1869, Virginia established its free school system in 1870. The first state superintendent, H. R. Ruffner, was appointed on March 3, 1870. [35] He was a southerner whom historians, in general, regard as having been very liberal in his approach to educating Blacks.

Superintendent Ruffner's first annual report, for the school year ending August 31, 1871, reflects that there was a disparity in the relative number of white and Black schools --which was considered to be due to the difficulty of finding qualified teachers for the Black schools. It was also observed that "... juster views concerning the honorable character of educating the colored people are becoming more prevalent every day. "[36]

At the end of the first year of the operation of the public school system in Virginia, the general educational outlook was so appalling that the United States Commissioner of Education, John Eaton, Jr., recommended that the federal government use proceeds from the sale of public lands to assist Virginia, and other southern states, in establishing and maintaining schools for universal education. He expressed dismay at the high percentage of children, Black and white, growing up in ignorance and pledged to do something about the situation. [37]

The following figures depict the population census and statistics of school attendance of Virginia in 1870: [38]

Table 1

STATISTICS OF SCHOOL ATTENDANCE IN VIRGINIA, 1870

White population, in 1870	712,089
Black population, in 1870	512,841
Total Virginia population census, in 1870	1,224,930
The number attending schools in 1870, reported by families	
Whites	59,792
Blacks	11,079
Total	70,871
Percentage of white attendance	8.39
Percentage of Black attendance	2.16
Percentage of Black and white attendance	5.78

The following figures depict comparative statistics on illiteracy in Virginia, in 1860 and 1870:[39]

Table 2

ILLITERACY IN VIRGINIA, 1860 AND 1870

Black population in 1860	490,865
White population in 1860	1,047,299
Total population	1,586,206
Black population in 1870	512,841
White population in 1870	712,089
Total population	1,224,930
Estimated number of whites over twenty, who were unable to read and write, in 1860	48,915
Estimated number of Blacks over twenty, who were unable to read and write, in 1860	208,000
Total	256,915
Percentage of illiteracy of whole population	21
Census figures of whites over twenty-one, who were unable to write, in 1870	67,997
Census figures of Blacks over twenty-one, who were unable to write, in 1870	207,595
Percentage of illiteracy of whole population	22.5

It will be observed that the overall illiteracy situation in Virginia shows a reversal from 1860 to 1870, yet Virginia moved very slowly to meet its educational needs, particularly with the Black population.

Many of the Virginia ex-slaves had been attending Freedmen's schools since 1861, when the first school was established at Fortress Monroe. Some had advanced considerably over the nine years to 1870, when Virginia started its public school system, but no provision was made by the state to provide them with secondary schools beyond those that existed then. There were more than nineteen secondary schools in Virginia in 1870, but only three of which Blacks could attend. Two of them were rated as institutions of higher learning and one as a secondary school. Hampton Normal Institute, founded in 1867 by the American Missionary Association, and Virginia Union University founded in 1865 by the American Baptist Home Mission Society, were institutions of higher learning that had secondary-education programs to facilitate input of students who were deficient in certain courses into their higher-learning programs. The secondary school, Colored High and Normal School, at Richmond, was founded by the Freedmen's Bureau in 1867.

Considering that there were only three schools offering secondary instruction for Blacks in 1870 and there were nearly twelve thousand Black students in elementary school, it is obvious why the Virginia Baptist State Convention considered secondary education to be of prime importance.

Summary

Feeling confident that it had a friend in President Andrew Johnson, Virginia, in keeping with its traditional prejudices, maintained strong opposition against the realization of two of the Blacks' most pressing objectives: to become full-fledged citizens and to educate their children. Legislating a set of Black codes similar to those first enacted in Mississippi in 1865, Virginia restricted the personal mobility of Blacks to the maximum extent possible during Reconstruction. It stopped just short of enslaving Blacks once again. All of this despite the federal Civil Rights Law, the Thirteenth and Fourteenth Amendments to the Constitution, and other social-welfare enactments that proved to be, in most instances, but empty words.

And so the Black code of Virginia replaced the slave

code and therein relegated Blacks to a different form of sub-jugation. Then too, to keep Blacks in their place, unruly, hostile molesters preyed upon them unremittingly. Not even the federal government, which had guaranteed the full rights of citizenship under the Fourteenth Amendment to the Consti-tution of the United States, was willing to enforce the laws to ensure Blacks their rights.

Although the Reconstruction period was filled with op-pression for the Black race, it did provide opportunity for a few of them to receive some education, thanks to the Freed-men's Bureau and to philanthropic and denominational groups. The state of Virginia was negligent in the execution of its responsibility to the Black race in that it made no effort to provide educational assistance through which the race could become more productive in society.

As Reconstruction came to a close in 1877, under the administration of President Ulysses S. Grant (Andrew Johnson had been impeached on May 26, 1868), Blacks had consider-able anxiety about their welfare. They knew that their exper-ience during Reconstruction was atrocious; they were dubious about the future.

Nevertheless, Black organizations, such as the Vir-ginia Baptist State Convention, were not ready to take a de-featist attitude. They knew that in the future they must dou-ble their efforts to bring education at all levels to their peo-ple, and this they were determined to do.

IV. SECONDARY SCHOOLS ESTABLISHED AND SUPPORTED
BY BLACK BAPTISTS IN VIRGINIA, 1887-1957

Introduction

The first secondary school founded by the Black Baptists of
Virginia was the Virginia Seminary. During the Twentieth
Annual Session of the Virginia Baptist State Convention, held
May 1887 in Alexandria, the membership adopted a resolution
to establish a school at Lynchburg. The school was incor-
porated on February 24, 1888, under the name of Virginia
Seminary, by an act of the state's General Assembly. The
unyielding determination and perspicacity of the leaders of the
Virginia Baptist State Convention enabled it to overcome many
obstacles to make this noteworthy achievement.

From the beginning at Lynchburg, the Black Baptists
of Virginia extended their educational efforts to give rise to
twelve additional secondary schools through 1907: Spiller
Academy, was founded at Hampton in 1891; the Ruffin Academy,
at Cauthornsville in 1894; the Northern Neck Industrial Academy, at Ivondale in 1898; the Keysville Mission Industrial
Academy, at Keysville in 1898; the Halifax Industrial Institute,
at Houston in 1901; the Rappahannock Industrial Academy, at
Ozeana in 1902; the Pittsylvania Industrial, Normal, and Collegiate Institute, at Gretna in 1903; the Bowling Green Industrial Academy, at Bowling Green in 1903; the King William
Academy, at King William Court House in 1903; the Fredericksburg Normal and Industrial Institute, at Fredericksburg in
1905; the Nansemond Collegiate Institute, at Suffolk in 1905;
and the Corey Memorial Institute, at Portsmouth in 1906. [1]

The history of Black-supported secondary schools in
Virginia would be incomplete without acknowledging the outstanding contributions that two schools of higher education
made toward making Black secondary schools possible.   They
are Virginia Union University and Hartshorn Memorial Institute,

both of which were founded at Richmond by the American Baptist Home Mission Society.   Both schools played significant roles in that they provided a large corps of leaders who were instrumental in giving rise to the Black secondary education thrust in Virginia in the late nineteenth century.

Though the Black Baptists of Virginia were not directly responsible for the births of Virginia Union University and Hartshorn Memorial Institute, they rendered financial assistance to both schools on a large scale.   The Virginia Baptist State Convention began supporting Virginia Union University financially shortly after the Convention was organized in 1867. It began supporting Hartshorn Memorial Institute in 1884, when that school was founded.   A majority of the male members of the Convention were ministers who were former members of Virginia Union University, while some of the female members were former students of both Virginia Union University and Hartshorn Memorial Institute.   Each group was loyal to its respective school and promoted its financial support at every opportunity.   In fact, Black Baptists across the state of Virginia had a high regard for both schools and helped to support them.

Virginia Union University, 1865-

Virginia Union University was founded at Richmond by the American Baptist Home Mission Society in April 1865, shortly before the city surrendered.   One teacher was sent there with the responsibility for opening a school for the Black children of the city as quickly as possible.   The one teacher performed his work so well that within a short time after the surrender of Richmond, the teaching force was enlarged to eleven.   In late November 1865, the Society sent Rev. J. G. Binney, formerly president of Columbian College (now George Washington University), Washington, D. C. , and later a teacher at Rangoon, Burma, to Richmond to teach Black children who desired to prepare for the ministry.   His first class consisted of twenty-five men who met with him at night, as they were forced to work during the day for survival.   After about eight months, around June 1866, Rev. Binney left the school and returned to Burma, where he became president of the Karen Theological Seminary.   He had left in disgust because he was not well received by the whites of Richmond and was unable to make suitable accommodations for his students. [2]

The next attempt to educate Blacks at Richmond was

made by the National Theological Institute and University in
conjunction with the American Baptist Home Mission Society.
The National Theological Institute and University was founded
at Washington, D. C. , in December 1864 to "train men of God
for the Christian ministry. " To carry out this objective the
organization established schools at important points where
ministers could be trained with the least interference to their
work.   The institution also conducted workshops for ministers
who were unable to attend school.   The attempt was made to
reach the masses of the Black ministry.   As a part of the
program, Rev. Nathaniel Colver, D. D. , Professor of Biblical
Theology at Chicago Theological Seminary, was employed by
the National Theological Institute and University to continue
the effort to educate Black ministerial students at Richmond.
He arrived in Richmond on May 13, 1867, and made arrange-
ments to start his work.   On July 1, 1867, he leased for
three years, at one thousand dollars per year, an establishment known as "Lumpkin's Jail, " for a school site.   The establishment, which was formerly a slave pen, consisted of
four brick buildings.   One was used by the former proprietor
as his residence and office; another as a boarding house for
slave traders; another as a barroom and kitchen; and the fourth
was the old jail where slaves were housed until they were dis-
posed of at public or private sale.   The owner, a white man,
had a Black wife who bore him several daughters, all of whom
he sent North to be educated. [3]

Early in July 1867, a "school of colored prophets" was
gathered at the old jail site to begin their educational work.
They were taught by Dr. Colver, who for twenty-eight years
was the president of Richmond College (now the University of
Richmond) and for twenty-five years pastor of the First African Baptist Church, Richmond.   By the end of November there
were eighty-eight students in attendance, including thirty-six
day, thirty-seven night, and fifteen primary students.   Twenty-
five of the men were enrolled as ministerial students. [4]

In addition to the regular curriculum, special seminars
of four and five weeks were held occasionally by Dr. Colver
and his staff.   The seminars were on such topics as church
organization, ministerial duties in regard to the Sunday School,
church discipline, marriage and divorce, benevolence, plans
for sermons, and Christian doctrine.   Discussions were generally led by Dr. Colver, assisted by Dr. Robert Ryland and
other missionaries from the National Theological Institute and
University.   The efforts made by many Black ministers to get
to the school, according to Dr. Miles Mark Fisher, reminded
one of the mendicant friars of medieval Europe.   He said:

> Some came one hundred and fifty miles, most on
> foot, begging their bread as they came, and turning
> into cabins for shelter in the night. Some borrowed
> the clothes they wore, a vest of a cousin, pants of
> a brother, and a coat of a father. So the whole
> neighborhood contributed to the wardrobe of a preach-
> er, the whole outfit worth less than five dollars....
> They ranged in age from 24 years to 60, but they
> traveled to Richmond, learned, and then returned to
> their respective locales to preach to thousands. [5]

Dr. Colver was seventy-four years of age and in failing health when he went to Richmond. That did not deter him,
however, as he organized and led the early development of the
Missionary school at Richmond. By the spring of 1868, just
as he was getting his work systemized, his wife's health made
it necessary for him to return to Chicago. Mrs. Colver died
on April 18, 1868. Dr. Colver, old and infirm, and stricken
with grief, returned to his post at Richmond, but was unable
to carry on his work. He, with Dr. Ryland, resigned the
work at the school in June 1868. Dr. Colver resigned due
to ill health and Dr. Ryland to an overload of work. Colver
left a lasting impression on all with whom he came in contact. His work at Richmond placed the school on a foundation
that was to be developed on by generations to come. His work
was so outstanding that the National Theological Institute and
University adopted a resolution on January 22, 1869, that gave
the school its first name, "Colver Institute. "[6]

In September 1868, Charles Henry Corey, D. D. , was
transferred to Richmond from Atlanta, Georgia, to carry on
the work started there in 1865 by Rev. Binney and then carried forward by Drs. Colver and Ryland. During his administration, changes took place rapidly in the development of the
Colver Institute. [7]

On May 19, 1869, the Board of Managers of the National Theological Institute and University transferred all of
their responsibilities to the American Baptist Home Mission
Society. The Society immediately accepted full responsibility
for Colver Institute and made plans to expand its operation.
On January 26, 1870, Dr. Corey relocated the school from
the "Lumpkin's Jail" site to a building that had been occupied
by the United States Hotel on the corner of Nineteenth and
Main Streets. The building was adequate for school purposes,
as it contained fifty rooms, several of which were auditoriums
in which ministerial students could practice. Less than one

month after the school was relocated, it was redesignated.
The name was changed from Colver Institute to Richmond Institute and incorporated by an act of the General Assembly.
The name Richmond Institute became the first officially recognized designation of the school by the state of Virginia.   There
were nine trustees named in the charter when the school was
incorporated, three of whom were Black. [8]

Under the direction of the American Baptist Home Mission Society, and supported by the Virginia Baptist State Convention, the work of the Richmond Institute grew so rapidly
that it soon became apparent to the Baptist leaders that a
broader program for Blacks, who aspired to become ministers,
was needed.   The leadership was interested in a distinctively
theological institution at Richmond.   They were convinced that
the increasing intelligence of the Black race and the interest
it manifested in the profession, made it a necessity.   It was
thought that Richmond was the best place for a theological
school, as it was centrally located. [9]

On June 28, 1880, under the administration of Dr.
Corey, a new site, consisting of two and one-half acres, was
purchased in the western section of Richmond.   Business sur-
roundings at the old location made the hotel building undesir-
able for further school purposes.   Moreover, the Board of
Trustees of Richmond Institute considered plans to build a
higher theological institution to which the advanced students
from all schools could come to complete their studies. [10]

When the American Baptist Home Mission Society held
its Fifty-First Annual Session at New York City in December
1883, it resolved to effectuate plans for the higher theological
institution at Richmond by the fall of 1884.   It was also decided that the Society would make an especial appeal to philanthropists for financial support of the school. [11]

In 1884, by request of the Society, the General Assembly of Virginia passed an act that changed the name of Richmond Institute to Richmond Theological Seminary.   Fifteen
years later, in 1899, Wayland Seminary, a secondary school
for Blacks who desired to prepare for the ministry, at Washington, D. C. , was merged with the Richmond Theological
Seminary to become Virginia Union University.   The school
was then organized into four departments; Elementary, Secondary, College, and Theology. [12]

From 1868 to 1882, Richmond Institute had a cumulative

enrollment of seven hundred and seventy-one, five hundred and thirty-two of whom were in the regular course. More than three hundred of them were Theology students, while about two hundred studied to become teachers. During the same period, according to statistics compiled by the Society, more than seven thousand persons were saved through the efforts of the students; many thousands were added to church rolls served by graduates; more than fifty churches were established; and about one hundred Sunday Schools were founded. One graduate baptized sixteen hundred persons into membership of the church he pastored in two years; another, thirty-three hundred. Two graduates became missionaries to Africa, one under the auspices of the Virginia Baptist State Convention and the other the (white) Southern Baptist Convention. [13]

Extracts of two of the many letters written by former students to Dr. Colver, President of Richmond Institute, attest to the work that was performed by former students, and the respect they had for their alma mater. Rev. Aaron Wells of Petersburg, who left the Institute in 1881, wrote on May 20, 1892:

> I have built three churches, established five Sunday Schools, and have baptized over one thousand persons.... For several years I was moderator of the Bethany Baptist Association, and president of the District Sunday School Convention. The influence of the school upon my spiritual life was what the influence of devoted and religious parents would be to their children. At the school I also learned to study. If my course of study has not drawn me closer to my people then I have made a great failure. I have reason to believe I have not made a failure. [14]

Rev. Richard Spiller, who left Richmond Institute in 1874, was pastor of the First Baptist Church and principal of the Spiller Academy, Hampton, Virginia, when he wrote to Dr. Corey on June 23, 1894:

> I attribute my success largely to the training I received at the Richmond Institute combined with the early training of my parents. The training I received in school has guided me all through my ministerial life, and it has a tendency to draw me nearer to the people and has taught me how to become all things to all people that I might save some. [15]

The sentiments expressed by Revs. Wells and Spiller, among many others, are no less true today relative to the esteem that former students hold for Virginia Union University. Throughout the history of this great institution, male and female students have been organized with high ideals and their consciences fired with anxiety to foster education and support the uplift of humanity. The school has always maintained a record of which it must be justly proud. No literary embellishments are necessary to glorify its achievements; the record indicates that it is the foundation upon which Black secondary education, as well as higher education, was developed in Virginia.

Many of the graduates of Virginia Union University became teachers, business persons, foreign missionaries, ministers, physicians, and lawyers. It is impossible to estimate the vast amount of good that has been done by the former students of this school, known successively as Colver Institute, Richmond Institute, Richmond Theological Seminary, and Virginia Union University. Prominent among the former students who have carried out the traditions of the school are the late Dr. William Lee Ransome, pastor-emeritus of the First Baptist Church, South Richmond, Virginia; the late Dr. Thomas Henderson, former president of Virginia Union University; the late Dr. John M. Henderson (Dr. Thomas Henderson's brother), former pastor of the Bank Street Baptist Church, Norfolk, Virginia; the late Dr. J. Marcus Ellison, President-Emeritus of Virginia Union University; Vice Admiral Samuel Gravely, Commander of the Third Fleet, United States Navy; Dr. William Holloman, former Director of Hospitals, New York City, and Chairman of the Board of Trustees, Virginia Union University; Dr. Allix James, former President, Virginia Union University; Dr. Wendell P. Russell, former President of Virginia State University, Petersburg, and Federal City College, Washington, D.C.; Henry Marsh III, Mayor of Richmond; and Dr. Samuel D. Proctor, Martin Luther King, Jr., Professor of Education, Rutgers University, New Brunswick, New Jersey, and Pastor of the nation's largest Black church, Abyssinia Baptist church, New York City. Dr. Proctor has distinguished his alma mater perhaps far more than any other former Virginia Union student. In slightly more than a half-century, he has served as president of two institutions of higher education, Virginia Union University, his alma mater, and the Agricultural and Technical College, Greensboro, North Carolina. Moreover, during the administration of President John F. Kennedy, he served as Associate Director of the Peace Corps.

Hartshorn Memorial Institute, 1884-1923

In the fall of 1879, the Virginia Baptist State Convention appealed to the American Baptist Home Mission Society to admit female students to the Richmond Institute. The Society approved the request and gave the Convention authorization to admit female students to Richmond Institute with the opening of schools in 1880. From 1880 to 1883, thirty female students attended the Institute, all of whom were trained as teachers. During the academic year 1884, however, there were no females enrolled at the Institute. The reason for the withdrawal of women was that Hartshorn Memorial College for girls had been established at Richmond in 1884, by the Rev. Joseph C. Hartshorn of Providence, Rhode Island, in memory of his wife. He gave twenty thousand dollars to the American Baptist Home Mission Society to purchase land and erect a school, and then gave the Society full responsibility for operating it. [16]

Hartshorn was a secondary school with a small elementary department designed to assist students who came poorly equipped to do secondary-level work. The purpose of the school was to train Black women to become teachers. To accomplish this, secondary subjects were taught in two courses, the "College Preparatory" or "Academic" and the "Normal."

The College Preparatory Course consisted of: three years of Latin; four of English; two of Mathematics; one of Elementary Science; four of Bible; one of Reviews; two and one-half of History; one-half of Agriculture; and one of Psychology. Electives were: Advanced Algebra; French; Education; and Methods and Practice Teaching. The Normal Course included three years of English; three and one-half of Mathematics; four of Bible; one-half of Agriculture; one-half of History; and one each of Educational Reviews and Practice Teaching. Normal Course electives were Latin, History, French, Ethics, Botany, and Education. Graduation from the Normal Department entitled the student to become certified by the state of Virginia to teach at the high school level. [17]

Dr. Lyman B. Tefft, a white clergyman, became the first president of Hartshorn Memorial Institute. He remained in that position until 1913, when he was replaced by Rev. George W. Rigler. The initial school population consisted of Rev. Tefft, six teachers, and seventy students. By 1916, the population had grown to fifteen teachers and one hundred and sixty-nine students. Twelve of the teachers were white and three Black. One faculty member was male and fourteen were

female.   All of the teachers were graduates of excellent
schools and highly proficient in their subjects. [18]

Many graduates of the Institute became teachers in the
Black public and private secondary schools of Virginia.   Through
affiliation with the Virginia Baptist State Convention and the
Baptist General Convention of Virginia (Baptist General Association of Virginia [Colored], some helped to establish Black
secondary schools in Virginia.

Major sources of funds for the school were tuition and
fees; the American Baptist Home Mission Society; the Woman's
American Baptist Home Mission Society; Black Baptists of the
State of Virginia; and donations from white churches. [19]

Hartshorn Memorial Institute, having operated successfully for more than forty years as an independent school, became the Woman's College of Virginia Union University in
1923. [20]

<u>The Virginia Baptist State Convention and the Emergence
of the Virginia Seminary, 1884-1899</u>

Despite its many problems, the Virginia Baptist State Convention performed outstandingly on all fronts, and grew phenome-
nally during the last quarter of the nineteenth century.   Considering that the Convention consisted predominantly of ex-
slaves, or the children of ex-slaves, it is a great tribute to
the leaders who guided the organization.   Many of the members were also former students of Richmond Institute and were
inculcated with Christian principles and ideals.   In fact, all of
the presidents, and most of the vice-presidents of the Virginia
Baptist State Convention, from its inception in 1867 to 1899,
when a schism occurred, were former students of Richmond
Institute.   All of them possessed an unyielding determination
to contribute to the advancement of the Black race, and persevered to that end.

When the Virginia Baptist State Convention held its
Seventeenth Annual Session at Staunton on May 11, 1884, it
passed a resolution to give a high priority to the education of
Blacks in the state.   To plan for the execution of this resolu-
tion, a special Educational Board was organized, with Rev.
Philip Fisher Morris, pastor of the Court Street Baptist
Church in Lynchburg, as the Chairman.   The city of Lynch-
burg was designated as the base of operation for the Educa-

tional Board.   Rev. Morris, a graduate of the Howard University School of Divinity, was well qualified for the job of Chairman.   He was a man of action, known throughout the state for
his aggressive leadership, loyalty to fundamental principles,
and high standards.   The Black Baptists of Virginia were satisfied that he was the right person for the position and confident that under his leadership the Board would make considerable progress. [21]

        At the Twentieth Annual Session of the Convention, held
at Alexandria in May 1887, Rev. P. F. Morris, Chairman of
the Educational Board, introduced plans for the organization to
establish and maintain its first secondary school (see above,
p. 41).   It was suggested that the school be opened at Lynchburg and be made a direct affiliate of Richmond Institute to
become a feeder institution to that school.   The proposal was
adopted immediately, and permission was given the Educational
Board to proceed to incorporate the proposed school.   Following instructions given by the Convention membership, the Educational Board of the Convention had the school incorporated
under the name of Virginia Seminary by an act of the General
Assembly of Virginia on February 24, 1888. [22]

        Virginia Seminary opened its doors to students on Janu-
ary 13, 1890, under the presidency of Rev. P. F. Morris,
with thirty-three students enrolled.   A frame structure, con-
taining two rooms, twenty-five feet by twenty-five feet, was
used as a temporary academic building, while a large building
designed for both administrative and dormitory purposes was
being erected.   The emergency building was barely able to
house the classes.   There were no boarding and sleeping facilities contained in it.   Students who came from beyond the
city of Lynchburg had to secure room and board with families
in the city.   With six acres of land valued at eighteen hundred
dollars, two part-time teachers, thirty-three students, and a
frame building with two classrooms, the Virginia Seminary began its uphill fight for existence. [23]

        Less than three months after the Seminary opened, it
encountered its first serious obstacle.   On April 12, 1890,
Rev. H. H. Mitchell, Corresponding Secretary and General
Manager of the Board of Managers of the Seminary, issued an
urgent appeal to the Black Baptists of Virginia for financial
support of the school.   In a letter published in the Richmond
Planet, a Black-owned newspaper in Richmond, he asked that
all Black Baptist representatives who planned to attend the
Twenty-Third Annual Session of the Convention, which was to

be held at Bedford, May 14-20, 1890, bring large sums of
money to keep the Seminary open.   He wrote that "the Seminary's future depends largely on what you do this year. "[24]

Unfortunately, Rev. Mitchell's appeal did not bring a
good response. This forced the Board of Managers of the
Seminary to appeal directly to the Convention members at
Bedford and ask for emergency assistance to resolve the financial crisis.   It was disclosed at the Convention that the
net worth of the school was $12,861.82, with an indebtedness
of $4,440.71 against that.   The main building of the school
was incomplete and in order to complete it the indebtedness
had to be liquidated first.   The Convention, through a resolution, empowered the Board of Managers to raise the necessary
money, either through borrowing it or issuing bonds. [25]

The day following the close of the session at Bedford,
on May 20, 1890, the Board of Managers of the Seminary met
and decided to make no further moves to build or purchase
supplies and equipment until the indebtedness of $4,440.71 was
liquidated.   It was decided too that once again a direct appeal
would be made to the Black Baptists of Virginia to come to
the financial aid of their school.   This time, however, the
Corresponding Secretary was advised to send a circular letter
to each member church of the Convention detailing the specific
financial need for survival.   Churches were to be apportioned
an amount of the debt based on their membership and asked
to pay within sixty days, or as soon thereafter as possible. [26]

The second appeal went out to the churches within a
few days after the Board of Managers made its resolution.
Once again, it met with the same fate as did the previous appeal in the Richmond Planet. President Morris was highly
displeased that the Black Baptists did not respond to the rally.
He thought that through the negative response, Black Baptists
of Virginia demonstrated a genuine lack of confidence in the
administration and interest in the school.   On that basis, he
made a direct appeal to the American Baptist Home Mission
Society for financial assistance.   He wanted to keep the school
alive and was not concerned that should the Society subsidize
the school, control over the institution would go to the Society.
In early 1891, after repeated appeals, the Society acquiesced.
It notified President Morris and the Educational Board of the
Convention that it was willing to enter into a formal agreement
in regard to supporting and operating the Virginia Seminary. [27]

During the Twenty-Fourth Annual Session of the Convention, held at the First Baptist Church in Charlottesville in May 1891, the membership entered into a formal "Compact" with the Society relative to the Seminary. The "Compact" stipulated that in exchange for financial support of the school, the Convention agreed to allow the Seminary to become an affiliate of the Society with the control and management remaining with the Board of Trustees of the Seminary; the faculty would consist of only those persons approved by the Board of Trustees, subject to approval by the Society; and the President was to submit monthly financial reports to the Society showing all receipts and disbursements. [28]

Satisfied that he had saved Virginia Seminary from financial disaster, yet saddened because he had not received adequate financial assistance from the Black Baptists of Virginia, Rev. P. F. Morris resigned from the Presidency of Virginia Seminary immediately after the Compact was ratified by both parties. He had hardly finished resigning when a bitter fight began in the Convention meeting that resulted in "splitting the Virginia Baptist State Convention into two separate schools of thought. " One group of representatives advocated cooperating with the Society and the other was adamantly opposed to receiving any financial help from whites. The latter group wanted to maintain the Seminary as a racially independent entity. Little did Rev. Morris realize then that he had engineered an agreement that would eventually bring about a split in the ranks of the Black Baptists that would endure for many years to come. [29]

President Morris was succeeded by Gregory W. Hayes, an instructor of "Pure Mathematics" at the Virginia Normal Institute (colored), Petersburg. Hayes was chosen for the position by the Board of Trustees of the Seminary while in attendance at the Twenty-Fourth Annual Session of the Convention. The selection of Hayes was made within a brief period after the resignation of Rev. Morris was accepted by the membership. [30]

Gregory W. Hayes was born of slave parents in Amelia County, Virginia, September 8, 1862. Soon after his birth, his parents moved to Richmond, where he grew up attending the public schools. As a boy, Gregory Hayes had a hunger for knowledge that made him a conscientious and persevering student. Upon finishing the public high school at Richmond, he attended Oberlin College in Ohio, where he was graduated with a baccalaureate degree, and finally, in 1888, with Master of Arts degree. When he became president of Virginia Seminary, he was only twenty-nine years of age. [31]

Upon assuming presidential duties at Virginia Seminary, in late 1891, Hayes discovered that his work was hampered by many disadvantages, among which were the Compact feud and the large indebtedness. Furthermore, the work on the main campus building was half completed and at a standstill. The Convention was unable to render financial assistance, as its treasury was depleted. The churches had made it known that they were either apathetic to the cause or otherwise unable to help, based on their response to the appeals made on earlier occasions. The only sure income for operation of the Virginia Seminary came from the American Baptist Home Mission Society, based on the Compact arrangement. President Hayes, a "race-man" through and through, was faced with a dilemma. [32]

Gregory W. Hayes was a layman and former Presbyterian. As part of the contract he accepted to become President of Virginia Seminary, he was converted to the Baptist faith by Rev. Zacheus Dearborn Lewis of Richmond and made a member of the Second Baptist Church of that city. This was done to satisfy those Convention members who were opposed to a non-Baptist becoming head of a Baptist school. President Hayes quickly became a good Baptist as he began to hammer away at removing the sickness from a dying institution. He quickly gained the respect and admiration of Black people throughout the state of Virginia, particularly Baptists, as though he was the great hope for a disappearing dream. The financial report he rendered to the Convention in 1894 shows that he had received $6,261.63 from various organizations to support the school. This figure does not include the funds contributed by the Society, which was also largely responsible for the new interest being shown in the Seminary. This is evidenced by a statement President Hayes made in March 1895 in the Mission Monthly Magazine, a publication of the Society, that the institution had taken on a new life under the inspiration of a gift by the Society of eleven hundred dollars yearly, in 1891, 1892, and 1893. Through the combined efforts of Hayes and the Society, enrollment increased from the initial thirty-three students, in 1890, to four hundred and eight by 1894. [33]

As the Virginia Seminary moved forward under President Hayes, the conflicting views, which arose as a result of the Compact of 1891, became intensified. Hayes made it known beyond a doubt that he was a staunch advocate of racial independence. An orator of renown, he made frequent appearances before large audiences, at which he always espoused his personal racial philosophy. If he spoke to a young Black group,

he invariably encouraged them to become educated in order
that they might enjoy equal opportunities, as a race, with
other races in America.   He was so outspoken on the race
issue, particularly the matter of racial independence for the
Virginia Seminary, that the American Baptist Home Mission
Society made it known both to him and the Convention that it
would not tolerate him preaching racial independence while
the school was being supported by it.   The Society also reminded Hayes that it was knowledgeable that he was strongly
coercing Blacks to spurn the Compact and exercise control
over their own school.   The Mission Monthly carried an article that struck at Hayes for opposing the Society having super-
visory control over the Seminary while it paid his salary.   It
was also revealed that Hayes was at odds with the Society because he was strongly in favor of elevating the Virginia Seminary to college level.   This aggravated Society officials, as
they wanted the Seminary to remain at secondary level and
serve as a feeder institution to the Richmond Theological
Seminary, the Society's totally owned higher-level school in
Virginia.   Further, the Society had plans to make the Richmond Theological Seminary a large university complex, with
Virginia Seminary, Lynchburg, and Spiller Academy, Hampton,
becoming its primary outlying feeder schools.   Gregory
W. Hayes was, according to the Society, impeding progress. [34]

        Notwithstanding what the Society thought of President
Hayes as being an impediment to progress, the stringent efforts of Hayes and his supporters, the "Race-men," to keep
the Virginia Seminary racially independent, were futile.   When
the Twenty-Ninth Annual Session of the Virginia Baptist State
Convention convened at Norfolk in 1896, a resolution was unanimously adopted to enter into a new agreement with the Society to formally designate the Virginia Seminary and Spiller
Academy as affiliates of what was to become known as
Virginia Union University in Richmond.   Needless to say,
President Hayes and his supporters were upset at the
resolution.   Hayes openly disclosed that he would not abide by
it, as to do so would destroy the racial identity of the Virginia Seminary.   He not only refused to make reports to the
Society but began a personal crusade of contacting members
of the Convention and educating them on the dangers involved
in maintaining the Compact of 1891 and the affiliation agreement of 1896.   He used all the force of his eloquence to per-
suade members to act expeditiously to break both agreements
as quickly as possible.   He even went so far as to threaten
to organize the Baptists who supported him against those who

favored white support for Black education.   With full knowledge
that his livelihood depended on the American Baptist Home Mission Society, he persisted unswervingly in his endeavors to
break the chains that bound the Seminary to the Society.   He
carried his efforts so far that finally, around 1898, the Society
threatened the Convention to release him or else.   Fortunately,
the decision was somehow set aside, and Hayes remained as
President. [35]

Although Hayes narrowly escaped being dismissed, his
ardent fight for racial autonomy did not abate one iota.   He
continued to pass out a tirade of oratorical thunder against
white supremacy.   Directly after he was censored in 1898,
he commenced combing the state again to gain support to
break the agreement at the forthcoming Thirty-Second Annual
Session of the Convention, to be held on May 10, 1899, at the
First Baptist Church in Lexington. [36]

After many years of fighting, President Hayes's efforts
finally had results in 1899.   Backed by his supporters, some
of whom wrote articles in the Richmond Planet explaining the
significance of his argument to Blacks, Hayes went to the
Thirty-Second Annual Session of the Convention at Lexington
prepared to do or die.   When the business concerning agreements with the American Baptist Home Mission Society reached
the floor, Hayes's followers acquitted themselves outstandingly.
They presented their case against the Society exercising control over the Seminary so well that the agreements were re-
voked by a large majority of members.   This absolved the
Society of further financial responsibility for the Virginia Seminary and the Seminary from affiliation with Virginia Union University.   As a result of the vote of revocation, so much bitter-
ness and confusion came about during the Session that the Convention became divided into two distinct groups: the "Race-
men," led by President Hayes; Rev. Richard Bowling, pastor
of the First Baptist Church, Norfolk; and Rev. Wesley F.
Graham, pastor of the Fifth Street Baptist Church, Richmond;
and the "Cooperationists," led by Rev. P. F. Morris, then
pastor of the Eighth Street Baptist Church, Lynchburg, having
moved to that church from the pastorate of the Court Street
Baptist Church, Richmond.   The Race-men stood for racial
independence, in support of Gregory Hayes's philosophy.   The
Cooperationists advocated that cooperation should take place
between the races.   Before the Thirty-Second Annual Session
adjourned, delegates who were racially independent inclined,
and in the majority, selected a slate of officers of Race-men
to serve on the Boards of Trustees and Managers for the Virginia Seminary. [37]

The meeting at Lexington in 1899 was the last time
that the Black Baptists of Virginia came together in a single
body on a common point of interest. Thereafter, the Black
Baptists were divided into two separate organizations: the
Virginia Baptist State Convention and the Baptist General Association of Virginia (Colored). The Virginia Baptist State
Convention membership consisted of Race-men, who supported
the Virginia Seminary as a racially independent school. The
Baptist General Association of Virginia (Colored) membership
consisted of Cooperationists, who supported the Virginia Theological Seminary and College (Virginia Union University). The
Association was formed by Reverends P. F. Morris and Z. D.
Lewis at the First Baptist Church, Richmond, on October 18,
1899, several months after Lexington. [38]

Although the erudite, tenacious Gregory W. Hayes was
not able to consummate his dream of moving the Virginia
Seminary beyond the secondary level, he managed to keep it
alive and thriving as long as he lived. President Hayes died
at Johns Hopkins Hospital on December 21, 1907, while still
in office as President of the Virginia Seminary. Although he
was a layman, he influenced the style and thinking of more
Baptist preachers than any other teacher in the State of Virginia, with the exception of J. E. Jones, who published the
widely read Virginia Baptist. In the light of what he accomplished in the short span of eight years, the Baptists will always have cause to wonder what might have been accomplished
had he lived a quarter of a century longer. [39]

Upon the death of President Hayes, his widow, Mary
Rice Hayes, succeeded him. Within two years, in 1909, she
was succeeded by J. R. L. Diggs, Ph. D. Doctor Diggs remained as the school administrative head for one year, until
1910, when he was succeeded by Rev. R. C. Woods, who remained President until 1926. According to Rev. William
Henry Rowland Powell, who replaced Rev. Woods in 1926 and
served until 1929, the Seminary reached its peak during Rev.
Wood's administration. Under President Wood's leadership,
three new buildings were erected, the School of Religion was
upgraded to a Theological Seminary, the school was accredited
as a college, and the name of the institution was changed to
the Virginia Theological Seminary and College. In 1929, Rev.
Powell was succeeded by Rev. Vernon Johns. Rev. Johns remained as President until September 1934 and was replaced by
Rev. Powell. Rev. Powell remained as President on this occasion for twelve years, through 1946. Through hard work and
dedication, he did an outstanding job of removing the indebted-

ness that was plaguing the school when he returned there in
1934. Dr. Powell attributed much of his success at Virginia
Theological Seminary to Rev. Richard Bowling, for many years
pastor of the First Baptist Church, Norfolk, and a staunch sup-
porter of Virginia Theological Seminary, recently redesignated
the Virginia College. Many thousands of dollars were raised
by Rev. Bowling to support the institution. Dr. Powell indicated that during his presidency no man was more outstanding,
among those who stood by him in willing service, in providing
financial assistance, advice, encouragement, and responses to
call, than Rev. Bowling. [40]

Virginia College operates today as an institution of
higher learning devoted to the same high ideals as it was when
founded at Alexandria in 1887. It is still under control of the
founding institution, the Virginia Baptist State Convention. [41]

The Baptist General Association of Virginia (Colored) (The Baptist General Convention of Virginia), 1899-

The Baptist General Association of Virginia (Colored) was organized at Richmond in 1899 by the staunch Cooperationists
who desired to carry out the Compact with the Society, which
had been rejected at Lexington in 1899. Their purpose for
organizing also included cooperation with the Southern Baptist
Convention, the Baptist Convention, the Baptist General Association of Virginia (White), and the American Baptist Publication Society. When the constitution of the Baptist General
Association of Virginia (Colored) was adopted, the cooperation
clause stated specifically:

> Cooperating with such other Baptist organizations
> for Christian benevolence as shall fully respect the
> independence and equal rights of the churches. [42]

The Association grew so rapidly that when it held the
Fourth Annual Session in October 1902 at the First Baptist
Church in Farmville, it was scarcely able to accommodate
the large delegation. There were represented one hundred
and nine churches, one hundred and forty-six delegates, three
associations, and six societies. The sum of $1,861.87 was
raised to be distributed for education and missionary work at
home and abroad. The main business conducted was the adop-
tion of a plan, submitted by the Executive Committee, which
was chaired by Rev. H. L. Barco of Portsmouth, to establish
nine academies. They were to offer both elementary and

secondary levels of training and come under the direct control
of the local Baptist associations within whose bounds they were
to be located.   It was also resolved that they were to be owned
fully by the Black Baptists of the state of Virginia, but also
were to become affiliates of the Baptist General Association
and encourage their graduates to attend Virginia Union University.   In return for accepting these conditions, the Baptist
General Association promised to give each academy at least
two hundred dollars annually.   The local Baptist Associations
accepted the plan and consented to execute it.   The American
Baptist Home Mission Society condoned the plan and offered
to give one thousand dollars annually to each school while it
was getting organized. [43]

The Baptist General Association Academy Plan entailed
establishing academies in rural areas throughout Virginia in
order to reach the Black masses that dwelled there.   One each
was to be located within the bounds of the Schaeffer Memorial
Baptist Association, Southwest, Virginia; the Northern Virginia
Baptist Association, Northern; the Northern Neck Baptist Association, Northern Neck; the Southside-Rappahannock Baptist
Association, south side of the Rappahannock River; the Norfolk
Union Baptist Association, Hampton; the Bethany Baptist Association, Suffolk; the Bannister Association, Houston; the Blue
Stone Baptist Association, Keysville; and the Northampton Baptist Association, Eastern Shore.   At the time the measure was
adopted, in 1902, four of the academies were operational and
affiliated with the Association.   They were: Spiller Academy,
Hampton, which was in the bounds of the Norfolk Union Baptist Association; the Keysville Mission Industrial Academy,
Keysville, in the bounds of the Blue Stone Baptist Association;
the Northern Neck Industrial Academy, Ivondale, in the bounds
of the Northern Neck Baptist Association; and the Halifax Industrial Institute, Houston, in the bounds of the Bannister
Baptist Association. [44]

In 1907, when the Baptist General Association held its
Ninth Annual Session at the Mt. Zion Baptist Church, Richmond, the Executive Committee reported that seven academies
were then operating under the general supervision of the Association.   The three academies that had been established since
the Farmville meeting, in 1902, were: the Rappahannock Industrial Academy, Ozeana, Essex County, in the bounds of the
Southside-Rappahannock Baptist Association, in late 1902; the
Pittsylvania Industrial, Normal, and Collegiate Institute, Gretna, Pittsylvania County, in the bounds of the Cherry Stone
Baptist Association, 1903; and the Corey Memorial Institute,
Portsmouth, Norfolk County, in the bounds of the Norfolk

Union Baptist Association, 1906. Corey Memorial Institute
replaced Spiller Academy, which had been in the Norfolk Union
bounds before the Convention relocated it to Cheriton, Northampton County, which was in the bounds of the Northampton
Baptist Association, and redesignated it Tidewater Collegiate
Institute. [45]

The King and Queen Industrial High School, which had
not been considered in the Baptist General Association's original academy plan, became an indirect affiliate of the organization in 1906. In that year, Rev. J. R. Ruffin, founder-
owner of the high school, deeded one acre of land and one
frame building to the Southside-Rappahannock Baptist Association in exchange for financial support of his school. The
Southside-Rappahannock Baptist Association was an affiliate
of the Baptist General Association of Virginia (Colored).

At the close of 1907, the Baptist General Association
controlled eight academies. It had given rise to seven of the
nine it contemplated, and the one academy, King and Queen
High School, became an affiliate through necessity. Not all
of the academies operated within the specific bounds of the
local Baptist Associations as was planned, but all functioned
to render secondary educational opportunity to the Black masses
in the rural areas as was desired.

An example of the financial support given the seven
academies it founded is contained in the Financial Statement
of the Executive Committee of the Association for 1907. It
reveals that $12,985.40 was expended that year for the acad-
emies as shown:

Table 3

FINANCIAL STATEMENT OF THE BAPTIST GENERAL
ASSOCIATION OF VIRGINIA (COLORED), 1907

Institution	Amount
Corey Memorial Institute	$1,800.00
Rappahannock Industrial Academy	1,491.83
Northern Neck Industrial Academy	1,750.00
Tidewater Collegiate Institute	2,879.76
Pittsylvania Industrial, Normal, and Collegiate Institute	1,595.23
Halifax Industrial Institute	508.00
Keysville Mission Industrial Academy	2,960.58
Total	$12,985.40

Of the total $12,985.40 contributed to the academies, $12,200.48 was given by the Blacks of Virginia through their churches. [46]

It is estimated that more than five thousand students were graduated from the seven academies, which were founded by the Baptist General Association, during the many years they were open. Further, approximately 60 percent, or three thousand, of the graduates attended institutions of higher learning. More than half of the three thousand, nearly sixteen hundred, were former students at Virginia Union University. [47]

In 1964, the Baptist General Association of Virginia (Colored) was redesignated the Baptist General Convention of Virginia, the title it has today. Since its inception in 1899, the organization has maintained close liaison with Virginia Union University, and will likely continue to do so. The Executive Director, Dr. Caesar Scott, maintains his office on the campus at Virginia Union University in close proximity to the office of the President. He serves as the coordinator between the Convention and the University and works diligently in the interest of recruitment and financial support for it.

Spiller Academy (Tidewater Collegiate Institute), 1891-1938

When Rev. Richard Spiller became pastor of the First Baptist Church in Hampton in 1888, he had visions of helping the large Black population there to become educated and self-sufficient. A graduate of Richmond Institute, Rev. Spiller carried with him to Hampton the ideal of helping others to improve themselves as instilled in him by Dr. Charles H. Corey and members of his staff. He saw a great need to help the Black people of Hampton, and quickly became engaged in doing so. Within three years after his arrival at Hampton, by early 1891, Rev. Spiller began to realize the fruits of his labor, when he organized, in the basement of the First Baptist Church, a Building and Loan Association for the Black citizens. Later, around October 1891, he organized a school that offered both elementary and secondary levels of education. He became principal of the school and named it after himself, Spiller Academy. Rev. Spiller remained principal of the Academy until 1895, at which time the Virginia Baptist State Convention, under whose supervision the school was founded, replaced him with Rev. George E. Read, another graduate of Richmond Institute and pastor of a large Baptist church at East Orange, New Jersey. Both Revs. Spiller and Read were Cooperationists, who, when the Baptist General Association of Virginia (Colored) was founded in 1899, became members of that organization. Support of the Spiller Academy then shifted from the Virginia Baptist State Convention to the Baptist General Association of Virginia (Colored). [48]

The main building of Spiller Academy was destroyed by fire in 1905 and the school was closed temporarily. In early 1906, at the request of the Northampton Baptist Association and the Eastern Shore Baptist Sunday School Convention, the Baptist General Association of Virginia (Colored) reopened the school at Cheriton, on the Eastern Shore of Virginia. Upon relocating the school at Cheriton, the Association redesignated it the Tidewater Collegiate Institute. [49]

Northampton County, in which Cheriton is situated, was entirely rural in 1906, with a total population of thirteen thousand. Over 55 percent of the total population, or seventy-six hundred were Black. There were a few public elementary schools available to Blacks in the county, but not nearly enough to provide adequately for their educational needs. The average length of the public school term was 8.1 months for white students and 6.3 for Black students. The number of teachers in white schools was fifty-six and twenty-five in Black schools. The average attendance was one thousand and thirty-three white students and seven hundred and sixty-one Black students. [50]

The site of the Tidewater Collegiate Institute was in the heart of a section where thousands of Blacks were concentrated, but were not exposed to educational advantages beyond attending the one-room, poorly equipped elementary school there. The Institute commenced operating in a new frame building, valued at two thousand dollars, on a two-acre tract. The building had been erected through the combined efforts of the Northampton Baptist Association and the Eastern Shore Baptist Sunday School Convention. [51]

Dr. Read, who was Principal of Spiller Academy when it burned at Hampton, resumed principalship at Cheriton when the school was relocated and redesignated. His wife, Annie, became his special assistant at Cheriton. She was a remarkable woman who worked alongside her husband constantly to bring improvement to Tidewater Collegiate Institute, the church he pastored, the African Baptist Church at Cheriton, and the community at large. [52]

Booker T. Washington visited the Tidewater Collegiate Institute in 1910 and praised Dr. Read and his staff for the work they were doing in the school and community. He commented:

> I very much wish we could bring to this country and community the teachers from every section of the south and let them come here and see what it is possible for people to do. You have a school and farm and other industrial work combined with religious work that is ideal, and I congratulate you, Dr. Read, teachers, and pupils, upon what I see here. 53

The second Principal of the Tidewater Collegiate Institute was Rev. Ulysses Grant Wilson, who succeeded Dr. Read in 1918. Rev. Wilson, a graduate of Virginia Union University, went to the Tidewater Collegiate Institute from the Bluestone-Harmony Academic and Industrial School at Keysville, Virginia, where he had served as Assistant Principal for several years. Upon his arrival at the Tidewater Collegiate Institute, he found it heavily indebted but yet in the process of building a large new physical plant, for which there was no foreseeable way to pay. Rev. Wilson, nevertheless, was undaunted. He accepted the challenge and assumed responsibility for carrying out the tasks of liquidating the indebtedness and completing the new buildings with zeal. Within a few years, the debts had been paid, the physical plant completed, the curriculum revised and improved, and the faculty strengthened. In the process of strengthening the faculty, Rev. Wilson employed several college-trained instructors, one of whom was his wife, Leah Marie. Mrs. Wilson, the former Leah Marie Freeman of Danville, Virginia, was a graduate of the Hartshorn Memorial Institute. She was a teacher of general subjects. 54

Evelyn Collins Brown, a 1921 graduate of the Tidewater Collegiate Institute, and teacher there from 1928 until 1934, recalled that Rev. and Mrs. Wilson, both of whom taught her three years, were outstanding personalities and extremely competent teachers. They were both hard workers who thought nothing of toiling far into the night to render assistance to their students. From the day he became Principal, in September 1918, until he left the institution in the summer of 1927, Rev. Wilson worked diligently to improve the environment at the Institute. A stoutly religious man, he relied heavily on organizing and conducting the Institute's educational program on the basis of Christian principles. Students and teachers were required to attend devotional services each Friday and church on Sunday. Religious issues were discussed in classes and at student gatherings. Students, and oftentimes visitors, were told that they should take advantage of every opportunity to get an education, as it' was the Christian thing to do. [55]

During Rev. Wilson's administration at Tidewater Collegiate Institute, the curriculum was upgraded and all students were required to take courses that would render them eligible for consideration for college admission. Required subjects were English, History, Mathematics, Latin, French, and Chemistry. Home Economics was required for all women. Survival was to the fittest, as the entire teaching staff consisted of very strict taskmasters. They gave daily home assignments and accepted no excuses if the work was not completed as required. Moreover, all students were required to participate in classroom discussions daily. If a student was unable to articulate to the satisfaction of the teacher, action was generally initiated to receive permission from Rev. Wilson to have the student repeat the course. With the knowledge that they were subject to this discipline, only a few students were required to repeat secondary-level classes in the history of the school. [56]

Though academic excellence received the greatest emphasis during Rev. Wilson's administration, extracurricular activities were also emphasized and encouraged. Each student was required to participate in some athletic activity, as tennis, basketball, football, volleyball, or baseball. The school, from its inception, had outstanding baseball teams, which frequently attracted spectators from throughout Virginia and part of Maryland. When the team played at Cheriton, there was generally a large crowd in attendance. [57]

Rev. U. G. Wilson was succeeded by Rev. J. R. Custis, a native of the Eastern Shore, in 1928. Rev. Custis, prior to returning to his native area, had pastored the Bethel Baptist Church in Franktown, Virginia, and taught at Portsmouth. Under his supervision, the Institute continued to progress on the same basis it did when Rev. Wilson was Principal. Rev. Custis was followed, in 1929, by George Edward Downey, an attorney and native of Accomac County, Virginia. Downey remained Principal of the school until it was permanently closed in 1938. The school was taken over by Northampton County in 1934, at which time it received financial support from both the county and the Rosenwald Fund. The school continued to progress under Downey as it did his predecessors. [58]

It is estimated that at the peak of its history, around 1931, there were more than two hundred and fifty students in attendance at the Tidewater Collegiate Institute. There were nearly one hundred in the secondary department. Approximately one hundred and fifty students lived either on the campus or with community members, some of whom were located as much as six miles from the school. Those who lived off campus walked to and from school daily, and never complained. They yearned for an education and dared not throw away the opportunity to attend Tidewater Collegiate Institute. It was a small price to pay by walking to school to improve themselves. [59]

The students who attended the Tidewater Collegiate Institute were no more dedicated to obtaining their educational goals than were their teachers to helping them do so. Mrs. Brown relates a very interesting story that illustrates the dedication of the ten teachers who comprised the Institute's faculty in 1933. The school underwent a financial crisis that year, and neither the Northampton Baptist Association nor the Eastern Shore Baptist Sunday School Convention was able to pay the teachers their annual salaries of two hundred dollars each. The Baptist General Association of Virginia (Colored) rendered the school some financial support but the money had to be used to pay other operational expenses. The Institute no longer received financial assistance from the American Baptist Home Mission Society, so it was almost defunct. The teachers were made aware of the situation, in September, at the beginning of the academic year, and given the option to stay and work for room and board until such time as the money was raised, or seek employment elsewhere. Not one teacher left. They remained at their teaching positions and applied themselves as diligently as they had in prior years. Mrs. Brown stated that she does not recall having heard a single utterance of displeasure on the part of a teacher during the entire school term. Further, at the conclusion of the term, all of the teachers remained at the school and assisted the Association and Convention with raising money to support the school and on behalf of their own salaries. Their efforts were successful. Throughout the crisis period, the teachers did not seem to mind the personal inconveniences they suffered. It appeared as if they were so committed to the common purpose of helping their students become responsible, upright citizens, they were not concerned with themselves. [60]

Many are the excellent graduates who went forth from Tidewater Collegiate Institute to perpetuate the ideals instilled in them by such great leaders as Dr. Read, Rev. Wilson, Rev.

Custis, Attorney Downing, and Evelyn Collins Brown.   Some
excelled in farming, some in business, some in medicine,
some in law, and still others in professions too numerous to
mention.   Among the more prominent graduates are: Evelyn
Collins Brown, Richmond; Carl Trehern, physician, who lives
in Kentucky; I. J. Goodman, D. D., who lives in New Jersey;
J. C. Allen, physician, who lives at Eastville, Virginia; Harvey Press, physician, Chief of Radiology, Freedmen's Hospital, Washington, D. C.; and Henry Joynes, mortician, War-
renton, Virginia. [61]

Ruffin Academy (King and Queen Industrial High School), 1894-1922

James Robert Ruffin, the son of Arthur and Martha Ruffin,
was born in slavery at Owenton, Virginia, on November 11,
1860.   Soon after the Ruffins were freed, around 1865, through
thriftiness and the kindness of an ex-master, they acquired a
two-hundred-acre tract of land at Owenton, the largest Black-
owned farm in the county.

When James Robert Ruffin was six years of age, in
1866, his mother died, leaving him and an infant sister in the
care of their father.   The senior Ruffin did an excellent job
of raising both children.   At early ages, he impressed upon
both the value of hard work, education, and religion in their
lives.   Daily, through Saturday, he carried them to the fields
to work, when they were not attending the American Baptist
Home Mission Society Elementary School at Owenton.   Although
he had not been baptized, he carried his children to First
Mount Olive Baptist Church regularly. [62]

Several years after James R. Ruffin completed his elementary-level work, around 1878, he became acquainted with
George Mellen Prentiss King, D. D., President of Wayland
Seminary in Washington, D. C.   Dr. King, who was employed
by the American Baptist Home Mission Society, learned from
Society teachers at King and Queen County that young Ruffin
was very bright and interested in furthering his education to
become a Baptist preacher.   President King wrote to young
Ruffin and invited him to attend Wayland Seminary to take both
secondary and theological training.   James R. Ruffin accepted
the invitation and on or about September 1882 went to Washington and enrolled in Wayland Seminary.   After finishing the secondary work in 1885, he enrolled in the Theological Department,
from which he was graduated in June 1887. [63]

Immediately upon graduation from Wayland Seminary, Rev. James R. Ruffin returned home to help his father on the large farm. On Sundays, he traveled to various churches in the county, where he usually preached. In early 1888, he was called to pastor the New Morning Star Baptist Church, St. Stephen's Church, Virginia, which was not far from his home. Several months after he became pastor of the New Morning Star Baptist Church, he had the pleasure of baptizing his father, Arthur, who was then sixty-eight years of age. That same year, in October, James R. Ruffin married his childhood sweetheart, Martha Ellen Johnson, in the same church.[64]

From the onset of the Ruffin marriage, the couple dedicated themselves to bring educational and spiritual uplift to the more than five thousand Blacks who resided in the county, most of whom were illiterate. They were aware that Blacks represented more than 60 percent of the total county population and received no help from the county to remedy this deplorable condition. Had it not been for the church-supported elementary schools, the illiteracy rate in the county would have been much higher. The couple vowed to give their personal assistance to the alleviation of the illiteracy. They were determined to wait no longer for the white residents of the county to act in their behalf. To this end, in 1894, Rev. Ruffin erected two frame buildings on his father's farm, one of which was a combination elementary-secondary school and the other a girls' dormitory. The purpose of the combination elementary-secondary school was twofold. It was intended to provide an elementary education to those county residents who desired to become functionally literate, in the least, and a secondary education for other purposes. The school was named Ruffin Academy, in honor of Rev. Ruffin's parents, the father who lived and the mother who was deceased. In the same year, Rev. Ruffin also founded a post office, near his home, and designated it Cauthornsville. It was named in memory of a man who had lived in the community for many years, George Cauthorn. Cauthorn, a bachelor and devoutly religious man, had made many contributions to the advancement of the Black race in his community. Rev. Ruffin was impressed with what Mr. Cauthorn had done and named the post office in his memory.[65]

In 1894, Ruffin Academy was the only secondary-level school that Blacks could attend within a five-county area. Students attended the school from King and Queen, King William, Caroline, Essex, and Middlesex counties. While a few girls stayed on the campus, most students traveled there daily by ox cart, goat cart, horse, horse and buggy, horse and wagon, and on foot. Those students who stayed on campus for five days of the week were charged five dollars per month for room and board. Those who remained at the school for seven days were charged six dollars per month. [66]

When the Ruffin Academy opened in 1894, there were two teachers present, Rev. James R. Ruffin and Mr. James Gardiner, a graduate of Richmond Institute. Rev. Ruffin taught the secondary subjects while Gardiner taught seven elementary grades. The initial enrollment at the secondary level was six students. The first student of record at Ruffin Academy was Watson R. Harvey, a thirteen-year-old farm boy from King and Queen County, who enrolled in September 1894. Later in the fall, around November, he was joined by Misses Nancy J. Brooks, Luvenia Newbill, Julia Latney; and Messrs. W. B. Newbill and Thomas Gardiner. In 1900, four of the six, Misses Brooks and Newbill and Messrs. Newbill and Harvey, were graduated. They became the first graduates of the secondary level of Ruffin Academy. [67]

From 1894 until 1906, Rev. J. R. Ruffin maintained the Academy through funds received from students and provisions from his farm. Sometimes it was extremely hard to keep the school going, but he persevered and kept it open. In 1906, when students commenced attending the school from Pennsylvania, New Jersey, and Maryland, and enrollment reached an all-time high of seventy-five students, he was no longer able to carry the burden alone. He was forced to appeal to the local Baptist organization, the Southside-Rappahannock Baptist Association, for financial assistance. The request was considered favorably, and from that time forward the Association became involved in operating the Academy. Other changes also took place at the Academy during the same year. The school was renamed the King and Queen Industrial High School; several new buildings were erected to provide additional classroom and dormitory space; and teachers were added to the staff. [68]

In April 1908, Mary B. Jones, a resident of the Indian Neck community, King and Queen County, was graduated with honors from the King and Queen Industrial High School. Her academic record was so outstanding that Rev. J. R. Ruffin offered her a teaching position summarily. He asked her to teach general subjects at a salary of one hundred dollars for six months, with room and board. She accepted the offer and taught at the King and Queen Industrial High School during the academic year 1909-10. Thereafter, she went to college and then returned to King and Queen County to teach at various elementary schools for more than fifty years.   Jones's sister, Lea, was also a graduate of King and Queen Industrial High School, in the class of 1914.   She too taught for many years in King and Queen County. [69]

Teachers who served on the faculty at King and Queen Industrial High School, other than Rev. J. R. Ruffin, Thomas Gardiner, and Mary Jones, were: Rev. C. A. Lindsey and Miss E. W. Fields, Middlesex County; Emma Moss, Rev. S. B. Holmes, and Rev. W. R. Harvey, King and Queen County; and Rev. A. P. Young, Caroline County.   They were well-trained, dedicated people.   Moss and Fields were graduates of Hartshorn Memorial Institute in Richmond.   Revs. A. P. Young, Watson R. Harvey, and Samuel B. Holmes were former students at Virginia Union University.   Rev. Lindsey was a graduate of the Theology Department, Virginia Seminary, Lynchburg.   All of them worked beyond the call of duty to educate the young women and men who attended King and Queen Industrial High School. [70]

The curriculum at King and Queen Industrial High School was structured after the secondary curriculum Rev. J. R. Ruffin had been exposed to at the Wayland Seminary.   Courses were offered in Bible, Ethics, Philosophy, Physics, Chemistry, History, Sociology, English, Health, Spelling, Latin, Algebra, Industrial Arts, and Music.   Students were required to take sixteen credits at the secondary level to graduate, twelve required and four elective units. [71]

The major athletic activity at King and Queen Industrial High School was baseball.   After the Rappanhannock Industrial, Normal, and Collegiate Institute and King William Academy were opened, King and Queen Industrial High School competed against them in baseball frequently.   The main recreational activity on the campus was drilling.   The school had a six-piece band that played every afternoon for about thirty minutes while the student body paraded in front of the academic building.   Rev. Ruffin, who required the daily drill event, accompanied his teachers to the parade daily and had the students pass in review before them.   Every Thursday afternoon, after drill, students were required to participate in special activities that related to maintaining the person or the school.   The girl students were required to sew, or perform other chores, to satisfy their personal needs or the needs of the school.   The boys were required to cut wood or perform carpentry on the school buildings.   Occasionally, all students were required to assist in farming the Ruffin farm. [72]

Religion was a major factor at the King and Queen Industrial High School. Bible study was a required unit of study. Devotionals were conducted each morning through the week. Prayer meetings were conducted once weekly, usually on Wednesday nights. Students were also required to attend Sunday services at a local church of their choice. Most of them attended First Mount Olive Baptist Church, Owenton, which was within walking distance from the school. Then too, Rev. Ruffin was a member of the church and preached there frequently. Out of respect for their Principal, most students went to hear him preach. Revival was conducted at the church every February for a week, and the students were required to attend. At that time, most of the students who had not converted to Christianity did so. [73]

In addition to serving as Principal of King and Queen Industrial High School, Rev. Ruffin served as postmaster at Cauthornsville; operated a community grocery; farmed two hundred acres; organized and founded the First Union Baptist Church, Rexburg, Essex County, Virginia, in 1912; and assisted his wife with raising their eleven children, all of whom were college educated. He was truly a remarkable man, who was assisted and supported by an equally remarkable woman. Wherever Rev. Ruffin went, his wife was at his side to assist him in any way she could. She was his greatest source of inspiration in all of his endeavors. [74]

Prominent among the graduates of King and Queen Industrial High School are: Mary B. Jones, retired teacher, Indian Neck; William Alsop, religious leader and farmer, St. Stephens Court House; Albert White, farmer, West Point; Rev. James Green, retired minister, Laneview; Rev. Watson R. Harvey, retired teacher, minister, and farmer, Newtown; George B. Ruffin, member, School Board, Northumberland County; and the late Dr. H. M. Ruffin, minister, social worker, and teacher, King and Queen County.

Rev. J. R. Ruffin died at Cauthornsville in 1920 at sixty years of age. During his brief life he accomplished many significant things and established a rich heritage, one that yet lives in the hearts and minds of those with whom he came in contact personally, and others who have learned of his great deeds indirectly.

In 1922, two years after Rev. J. R. Ruffin died, King and Queen Industrial High School was closed permanently. The school authorities of King and Queen County built a training school for Blacks, the King and Queen County Training School.

Financial support for the county training school came from
the county and the Rosenwald Fund. This brought to a close
the twenty-eight-year operational span of the King and Queen
Industrial High School.

Northern Neck Industrial Academy, 1898-1934

In the last decade of the nineteenth century, the Northern Neck
Baptist Association, which was organized on September 29,
1877, in Richmond County, was faced with a serious problem.
There were more than sixteen thousand Blacks in the four
counties it served--Westmoreland, Lancaster, Northumberland,
and Richmond--and 35 percent were illiterate. [75] None of the
counties seemed concerned about the high illiteracy rate, nor
did they act to remedy the situation. Although Blacks were
in a majority in the four counties, the only schooling available
to them was being provided through a few denominational-
supported one-room elementary schools. Most of those schools
were situated inconveniently for the Black masses, and attendance was generally poor. Something had to be done to improve the low educational status of Blacks in the counties.
The Association, based on its experience with the negativism
displayed on the part of the four counties over the years since
slavery, decided to act on its own to initiate educational programs for Blacks. It conceived the idea to erect a combination elementary-secondary boarding school. The specific objectives of the Association's project were to reduce illiteracy
among Blacks in the four counties and to provide a secondary
facility for those persons who desired to obtain a higher education. Under the leadership of Rev. Levi R. Ball (1854-1917),
Moderator, the Northern Neck Baptist Association voted in
July 1898 formally to establish an institution and name it the
Northern Neck Industrial Academy. At the same meeting, the
Moderator appointed a committee, chaired by Rev. Jacob Robinson, Northumberland County, to select and purchase a site
on which to build the school. [76]

After searching for several months, the Site Selection
Committee found what they considered to be an ideal location
for a school. It was a former plantation, Oak Farm, which
consisted of one hundred acres of farm and timberland. It
was centrally located to the four counties and readily acces-
sible by both land and water. It was also located in an area
in which a heavy concentration of Black people lived. The old
plantation site had still other advantages. It contained several
old farm buildings in fair condition, ten acres of wooded land

ready for cutting, and thirty acres of cleared land in excellent
condition for farming. The Site Selection Committee recommended to the Association that it purchase the property, which
it did in 1899. Soon after the property was purchased, the
Association's Moderator appointed a Site Preparation Committee to prepare the site for a school as quickly as feasible.
Working beaverishly to prepare the site, the Committee, assisted by other Association volunteers, converted the old farm
buildings to classrooms and a boy's dormitory, built a girl's
dormitory, and tilled and planted the farmland. Within a little more than three years, the school was ready to be opened.[77]

The Northern Neck Industrial Academy opened its doors
to students on October 1, 1901. Rev. Allen Poe Cheek of
Northumberland County, Virginia was appointed the first Principal, while Rev. Levi Ball was elected by the Association to
serve as Chairman of the Board of Trustees.[78]

The physical plant of the Academy consisted of three
buildings: an academic building, a girls' dormitory, and a
boys' dormitory. Each dormitory had a sleeping capacity for
twenty-two students. The academic and boys' dormitory buildings were the converted farm buildings. The girls' dormitory
was erected through funds donated by member churches of the
local Association.[79]

Due to a large increase in enrollment, the Association
erected another boys' dormitory, Northumberland Hall, at the
Academy in 1907. It provided sleeping room for twenty students. Unfortunately, in 1912 Northumberland Hall burned,
and another building, two stories high, was erected to replace
it. The replacement building was named Rappahannock Hall
and it had sufficient space to accommodate twenty-four boys,
twelve on each floor. The building also contained office space
for the Principal and sleeping quarters for him, the Dean of
Men, and other male faculty members. Potomac Hall, the
girls' dormitory, which was built before the school opened,
housed the office of the Dean of Women, her quarters, and
the quarters of other female faculty members.[80]

The building-expansion program was not incidental. The
Association had observed that the enrollment at the Academy
was steadily increasing. It was known by the Association membership, and other persons concerned with the education of
Blacks, that the Black race was not receiving any better educational treatment in the state of Virginia in 1907 than it had
received since slavery ended, and the future did not appear

brighter. Virginia still maintained only six public secondary schools for Blacks. They existed many years prior to the turn of the century, and were located in the cities of Richmond, Petersburg, Lynchburg, Danville, Staunton, and Winchester. Not one was in attending distance to any of the four counties served by the Association. Then too, only four hundred and seventy-eight Black students attended those schools, while eight hundred and thirty-two attended the fourteen private secondary schools. There were not enough Blacks attending either public or private secondary schools in Virginia. The total number that attended was a mere handful of the more than sixty-eight thousand Blacks in Virginia who were eligible to attend. The building effort was for the purpose of making space available to as many Black students as possible, particularly those from throughout the state of Virginia. [81]

Although the Academy had not been accredited by the Virginia State Department of Education, it was approved by that agency in 1916 as a three-year high school and in 1924 as a four-year high school. Subjects taught in 1924 were consistent with those taught at other secondary schools in Virginia, public or private. The first year of high school consisted of Algebra I, English I, General Science, and History as an elective; the second year Algebra II, English II, Biology, History, and Latin; the third year Geometry, Physics, English III, and History as an elective; and the fourth year English IV, Civics, Mathematics, and Chemistry. Although the Academy was chartered as an industrial school, it offered absolutely no industrial training. [82]

By 1928, the Academy had an enrollment of nearly seventy-five students, resident and nonresident. It had grown so that the Women's Missionary and Educational Convention, an auxiliary of the Baptist General Association of Virginia (Colored), raised funds and built a spacious combination administration-classroom building. It contained several luxurious classrooms, additional office space, and a large auditorium with a seating capacity of three hundred and eighty. The auditorium contained a large stage that was used by both the Academy and the community for dramatic presentations. The auditorium was used by the local chapter of the National Association for the Advancement of Colored People for its monthly meetings. It was deemed advisable to hold meetings there because the school was privately owned. The Sheriff's Department did not go there to intimidate those in attendance, by taking license-plate numbers, as it did when they gathered at churches on the main highway. Due to the physical layout of the school, in a densely wooded area, personnel of the Sheriff's Department stayed away. [83]

Students were required to conduct Sunday School, Baptist Young People's Union, and Prayer Services on their own. Teachers were usually present, but assumed no leadership roles. The administration was of the opinion that if students were to become self-sufficient, self-sustaining individuals, they had to learn to assume leadership positions as quickly as feasible. It was the administration's position that the leadership experience students gained at the Academy would be highly advantageous to them in their lives beyond the institution. [84]

Northern Neck Industrial Academy did not receive a single endowment in its history. The school was funded by member churches of the Association and was supported throughout its history by those same churches, contributions from various organizations, and tuition. Credit must be given to the Shiloh Baptist Church, Fairfields, Northumberland County, for the outstanding support it gave the Academy from its founding to the day it closed. Under the pastorship of the Moderator of the Northern Neck Baptist Association and Chairman of the Board of Trustees of the Academy, Rev. Levi Ball, Shiloh gave many thousands of dollars to the Academy. [85]

In the early 1930s, students were charged $114.50 annually for tuition, room, board, and incidental fees. The school experienced its peak enrollment in 1934, the last year it was open, with nearly one hundred students. Even so, the income from tuition, room, board, and general fees was far too meager to keep the school open. The Association had to raise money to support the school that year as it had done in prior years when there was insufficient income to support the school. Sylvester C. Booker, a former Principal of the Academy, who served from 1929 through 1934, recalled that when he went to the school in 1929 it was having financial difficulty. The school was so destitute then that the teachers were paid only fifteen dollars of the fifty dollars monthly pay they were promised. Booker, his wife, and the remaining teachers and maintenance personnel worked through 1931 before they received all of the pay that was due them. They were determined to remain at the school and impart knowledge to the students as long as they received the necessities for survival. [86]

J. Marcus Ellison, Ph.D., a former Principal of the Academy who served from 1917 through 1919, and protégé of Rev. Levi Ball, asserted that the Northern Neck Industrial

Academy made excellent progress over the years, but made its greatest progress during the administration of S. C. Booker. According to Dr. Ellison, Booker gave the Academy "sustained leadership over a five-year period which was highly pervasive throughout the school and community. " He told of how the school served as the hub of community activities over the years, and how the lives of the people, of the four predominantly rural counties the Academy served, were centered on it and their churches. Whenever public events were held at the Academy, Black residents of the four counties turned out en masse. Such events as May Day, baseball games, and dramatic presentations drew overwhelming crowds. Blacks of the farm counties looked forward to those occasions with glee, and supported them to the very best of their financial abilities. [87]

In a special report to the United States Commissioner of Education in 1916, Dr. Thomas Jesse Jones described the Northern Neck Industrial Academy as a small rural school, not sufficiently important to visit for inspection. Dr. Jones, having been commissioned by the United States Bureau of Education to visit and report on the status of Black schools in the United States, did not consider the institution large enough or sufficiently important to warrant his visit. He either overlooked or disregarded the fact that the poor Black people of the Northern Neck had scrubbed floors, picked cotton, and performed various other tasks to raise nickles and dimes to educate their own children. His oversight is reprehensible. Blacks of the Northern Neck of Virginia had worked hard to educate their children to become better contributing members of the same government Dr. Jones represented. [88]

Although the enrollment at the Academy was never more than one hundred in any particular year, and the school was not accredited until 1934, it was an institution of very high quality and maintained a high academic standard at all times. Over the thirty-three years it was open, there were more than one hundred and ten graduates, most of whom became teachers in their respective communities. Some of the graduates are: Rev. and Mrs. Henry E. Green of Ivondale, class of 1912; Mary Manning, Richmond, class of 1933; Ella Smith Ball, Kilmarnock, class of 1908; Rev. Carrol P. Morris, Whitestone, class of 1918; Rev. W. D. Yerby, Baltimore, class of 1915; and Ruth Rich, New York City, class of 1920. [89]

The Academy terminated on May 31, 1934, under the administration of S. C. Booker. Richmond County authorities built a high school for Blacks, Richmond County High School, which opened on October 1, 1934, with S. C. Booker as Principal. He remained as Principal of the county high school until 1939, at which time he relocated to Richmond. [90]

Not long after the Academy was closed, the Northern Neck Baptist Association began selling portions of the school site. Proceeds from the sale were endowed to Virginia Union University, around 1939, in memory of the Academy. According to Dr. Ellison, the endowment is now more than nine thousand dollars. [91]

Keysville Mission Industrial Academy (The Bluestone-Harmony Academic and Industrial School at Keysville), 1898-1957

In October 1898, when the Bluestone Harmony Baptist Association, Keysville, Charlotte County, founded the Keysville Mission Industrial Academy, it knew that the illiteracy rate among Blacks in the county was very high and something had to be done. Blacks were in a majority in Charlotte County, with a population of eight thousand of a total fifteen thousand residents. Thirty-five percent of the Blacks who were ten years of age and over were illiterate, and the county made no provision to remedy the matter. The Association felt obligated to provide a school in which teachers could be trained to assist in reducing the illiteracy rate. [92]

The Academy was started in a one-room building known as "Mission Building." Three members of the Bluestone Harmony Baptist Association were at the forefront in getting the school open. They were J. H. Wilson, William H. Hayes, and S. L. Johnson, all of Keysville. Hayes became the first Principal, assisted by two female teachers. The initial enrollment consisted of about one hundred and eighty students, eighty-four of whom were at the high school level. The three teachers taught ten grades, seven elementary and three secondary. [93]

In 1913, Hayes was succeeded as Principal by A. J. Goode. During Goode's administration, in early 1914, the Academy was redesignated the Bluestone-Harmony Academic and Industrial School at Keysville. In November of the same year, a special representative of the United States Bureau of Education, Dr. Jesse Jones, visited the school and conducted a thorough survey of its operation. He found it populated by five teachers and fifty-eight students, thirty-seven of whom

were boarders and seventeen matriculating at the secondary
level. Although the physical plant had been enlarged to include a large two-story academic building with five rooms,
and a three-story dormitory for girls, the school was on a
decline. The enrollment was lower then than it was at the
inception of the school. The condition of the school was such
that Dr. Jones recommended to the Board of Trustees that it
be combined with the local public elementary school, which
had opened several years previously. [94]

The Board of Trustees of the school did not adhere to
Dr. Jones's recommendation. It did, however, in 1917, after
the official report of the visit was made public, replace Goode
with Rev. Marcellus Carlyle Rux, who had been a member of
the faculty since 1912. Rev. Rux, a native of Meherrin,
Lunenburg County, Virginia, was a graduate of the School of
Theology, Virginia Union University, in the class of 1912.
His first pastorate was the Union Baptist Church, Charlotte
County, in 1912. Immediately after he became pastor of
Union Baptist Church, he joined the faculty at the Keysville
Mission Industrial Academy as a teacher of Philosophy and
Religion. While teaching, he amassed an outstanding record.
He was highly respected by teachers and students for his in-
tellect and integrity. His record as an administrator was equal
to his record as a teacher. While serving twenty-eight years,
from 1917 through 1945, he was instrumental in raising the
academic standing of the school to a high level and increasing
the enrollment to two hundred and eighty-six students by 1941.
That was the peak year in the school's history, with two hundred and six students in high school and eighty in the elementary grades. Buildings were erected or improved and the
faculty was strengthened quantitatively and qualitatively. A
girls' dormitory was erected during his first year as Principal, in 1917, at a cost of fifteen thousand dollars. Under
Rux's leadership, the school became the first Black privately
owned secondary school to be accredited by the Virginia State
Board of Education. He was also responsible for initiating a
Minister's Study course at the school, which later was enlarged to become a branch of the National Minister's Institute.
The physical plant, which was highly deteriorated when he became Principal, was valued at more than $125,000, in 1946,
when he retired. [95]

In January 1946, Rev. Marcellus Rux retired from active service, due to ill health, after having served thirty-
three years teaching and preaching in Charlotte County. He
was succeeded by G. W. Blue as Principal of Bluestone-

Harmony Academic and Industrial School at Keysville in 1946.
In 1950, Blue died and was succeeded by C. P. Franklin,
who, after three years, resigned in 1953. The last Principal
of the school was Rev. C. H. Rhodes, who succeeded Franklin in 1953, and remained until the school was closed by the
Board of Trustees in May 1957. [96]

Although the Bluestone-Harmony Baptist Association
tried very hard to keep the school open beyond 1957, the serious enrollment decline precluded it from doing so. The Supreme Court decision of 1954, which ruled that segregated
schools were illegal, had considerable impact on the enrollment status of the school. Many students who were enrolled
at the Bluestone-Harmony Academic and Industrial School at
Keysville, transferred to Charlotte County High Schools as
quickly as they were accepted.

The closing of the school marked the end of fifty-nine
years of educational service rendered by Blacks for Blacks
in Charlotte County.

Halifax Industrial Institute, 1901-1914

In 1900, the Black residents of Halifax County numbered
19,272 (slightly more than half of the total county population
of 38,000) and had an illiteracy rate of nearly 50 percent.
The county provided no educational assistance to alleviate
this deplorable state. There were several elementary schools
in the county, but all were sponsored by denominational or
philanthropic sources. There were no secondary schools
available for Blacks within a three-county area. [97]

During the last quarter of the twentieth century, the
Bannister Baptist Association, which served Halifax County,
had a membership of well-trained ministers who were extremely education conscious. A large percentage of the
ministers had been trained at Virginia Union University and
were anxious to share their knowledge with others, as they
had been taught by individuals like Revs. Charles H. Corey,
George Rice Hovey, and Henry L. Morehouse. They were
anxious to see improvement in the educational status of Blacks
in the county and prevailed upon the general membership of
the Bannister Baptist Association to join them in doing something in that regard. The appeal was made for the Association to consider erecting its own combination elementary
secondary school at Houston. The membership of the Asso-

ciation consented, and plans were made to open a school the
following year. [98]

In September 1901, the Bannister Baptist Association
founded the Halifax Industrial Institute, at Houston. The first
teacher-principal of the school was Leroy Gilmore, the sole
member of the faculty. The physical plant, which consisted
of a large frame building on two acres of land, was valued
at thirty-three hundred dollars. The building contained twelve
spacious rooms, which were used as classrooms, office space,
and quarters for female students. The land had been purchased by the Association specifically for the purpose of a
school. The building was erected through funds provided by
member churches of the Bannister Baptist Association and
through voluntary labor by Association members. [99]

Halifax Industrial Institute became an affiliate of Virginia Union University and was to have served as a feeder
school to that institution. Unfortunately, it did not function
as planned. It was unable in its thirteen-year history to produce one secondary-level graduate. From 1901, when the
Institute was founded, to November 1914, when it was visited
by a special representative of the United States Bureau of
Education, Dr. Jesse Jones, it failed to progress beyond elementary status. Gilmore was teaching alone then, as he was
when the school was founded. In fact, the school had retro-
gressed in enrollment. There were approximately twenty students in the school in 1901, and there were seven enrolled
when Dr. Jones visited. Jones recommended that the school
be transferred to the public school authorities of the county. [100]

Reports of the United States Commissioner of Education and copious other research sources did not reveal information concerning Halifax Industrial Institute beyond 1914. It
is therefore assumed that the school ceased to function that
year.

Rappahannock Industrial Academy, 1902-1945

While the Baptist General Association of Virginia (Colored)
met at Farmville in May 1902 to formulate plans to establish
nine secondary academies, the Southside-Rappahannock Baptist
Association prepared to open its school at Ozeana in October
of the same year. Long before the Baptist General Association of Virginia (Colored) became aware of the dire need for
a school at Ozeana, among other places, the Southside-

Rappahannock Baptist Association had conducted studies in the three counties it served, Essex, Middlesex, and King and Queen, and arrived at the decision to establish another combination elementary-secondary school for Blacks. It knew that the Ruffin Academy at Cauthornsville, King and Queen County, did an excellent job of educating Black children, but it was full to capacity and far too distant from Essex and Middlesex counties. Then too, the Association had learned that nearly 30 percent of the 15,920 Black inhabitants of the three counties, who represented nearly 60 percent of the total population, were illiterate. Since the three counties had done nothing beyond giving permission to denominational and philanthropic agencies to open schools in their boundaries, the Association felt morally obligated to do something to lower the illiteracy rate. [101]

In late October 1902, the Southside-Rappahannock Baptist Association opened a school in the Angel Visit Baptist Church, near Ozeana. D. C. Rawley, a graduate of the Virginia Normal Institute, Petersburg (Virginia State College), was the first teacher-principal. The school was designated the Rappahannock Industrial Academy and maintained at the Angel Visit Baptist Church until 1907, at which time it was moved to a site the Association had purchased, Monte Vista Farm, at Ozeana, Essex County, which consisted of a hundred and fifty-nine and a half acres of land. The farm was purchased for twelve hundred dollars. The Association borrowed two hundred dollars from the Baptist Women's Convention to complete the purchase. In return for the money, the Association gave the Baptist Women's Convention twenty-five acres of land. This left the school with a hundred and thirty-four and a half acres, to which it eventually added another hundred and sixty-one acres, for a sum total of two hundred and fifty-nine and a half acres of land. [102]

The new site was ideal for a boarding school, as it contained more than forty acres of farmland, which was used to supply food for the resident students. The remainder of the school property was in timberland, from which trees were sold periodically to support the Academy.

When the Academy opened at the new site, as a boarding school, W. Edward Robinson, a liberal-arts graduate of Howard University in Washington, D. C., was appointed Principal to succeed D. C. Rawley, who was designated his assistant. Robinson, a native of Essex County, had gained a reputation as an educator in Virginia through teaching at several

private and county-supported schools.   He was recognized as
a highly intelligent, committed person.   Although the Association was pleased with Rawley's performance at the Angel Visit
Baptist Church school, it was elated to get Robinson, as he
had far greater experience.   General Johnson, who knew Robinson, said that the people responded to his leadership and
helped him make the Academy an excellent institution.   During Robinson's administration, the school reached the enrollment mark of one hundred, around 1910.   By 1934, when
Johnson became Principal, the enrollment had risen to nearly
two hundred students from eight states.   In 1941, there were
seventy-three high school students enrolled alone, according
to a report submitted to the Association.   The largest number
of teachers in the history of the school was ten, in 1941. [103]

The secondary-level curriculum was somewhat rigid in
the 1940s.   Subjects taught were: English for four years;
General Mathematics for two; Algebra for two; General Science
for one; Early European History for one-half year; Modern
History for one-half year; United States Government for one-
half year; Latin for one-half year.   Home Economics was required for girls, and Music was an elective. [104]

The official designation of the school, the Rappahannock
Industrial Academy, gave the impression that industrial arts
was being taught, but it was not.   In the entire history of the
Academy, not one course was offered in industrial arts.   When
the school was visited in April 1915, this very subject was of
concern to the visiting officials.   Dr. Jesse Jones, Special
Representative of the United States Bureau of Education, recommended to the Board of Trustees of the Academy that industrial training be made part of the curriculum. [105]

In an effort to produce well-rounded, well-educated
young men and women, each administration at the Academy
insisted that all students participate in extracurricular activities.   Available activities were gardening, sewing, dramatics,
athletics, and choir.   The approach gained results, as for
many years during the 1930s the Academy had outstanding
choirs that won the highest honors in the school district.   Students were also required to attend Sunday School and church
services on a regular basis. [106]

In early 1938, during the administration of General
Johnson, the Academy was accredited by the Virginia State
Board of Education as a four-year high school.   This gave
the school a new lease on life. [107]

Minister members of the Southside-Rappahannock Baptist Association were extremely proud of the Rappahannock Industrial Academy and offered their assistance to make it succeed at every opportunity. Most of them were graduates of institutions of higher education, as Wayland Seminary, Howard University, Virginia Union University, and Virginia Seminary at Lynchburg, and appreciated the value of increased learning to Blacks. They visited the Academy regularly and lectured to the students on the significance of doing their very best in their academic endeavors. Most of them rendered financial support to the Academy by taking up special collections for it at their churches practically every Sunday. Other members of the Association were concerned with the Academy also. To raise funds, many members held cake bakes, dinner sales, and other events. Other sources of funds for the Academy were: the Virginia State Sunday School Convention (Colored), the Women's Missionary and Educational Convention (Colored), and the Virginia State Baptist Young People's Union (Colored). Income from tuition, room, board, and timber sales was also used to support the school operation. [108]

In the early 1940s, the three counties, King and Queen, Essex, and Middlesex, built public high schools for Blacks. The attendance at the Academy began to decline rapidly, so much so that in May 1945, after forty-three years of continuous service, the school was closed. Jerry Hoffman, who succeeded General Johnson as Principal in 1942, was the last administrator.

A man who had great positive influence on the operation of the Rappahannock Industrial Academy was the late Dr. William Amos Young, for many years Moderator of the Southside Rappahannock Association and Chairman of the Board of Trustees, Rappahannock Industrial Academy. He was a dynamic educational and religious leader in the state of Virginia who was often at the forefront of civil causes.

Young was responsible for the building of the first public schools for Blacks in Essex County, where he was born and lived for nearly ninety-two years, and the adjoining King and Queen County. He also organized and executed a vast educational facility movement for Blacks in Essex County, where he taught for years.

A graduate of the Secondary Department of the Virginia Normal Industrial Institute, Petersburg (now Virginia State University), Young received the Bachelor of Arts degree from

Virginia Union University, Richmond, in 1918.   The Doctor
of Divinity Degree was conferred upon him by Virginia Union
University in 1957.

        Dr. Young pastored the First Baptist Church, King
and Queen County, Virginia for fifty-nine years.   During the
same period he also pastored the Angel Visit Baptist Church,
Essex County, for forty-nine years and the Mount Olive Baptist Church in Hustle for forty years.   Mount Olive Baptist
Church was the church in which he held membership for most
of his life, having joined it as a mere boy of twelve or thirteen.

        Education was highly regarded by Dr. Young.   As a
teacher in Essex County for almost fifty years, he preached
constantly the value of education.

        A dedicated, conscientious, and hardworking individual,
Young was an inspiration to countless people throughout the
nation.   He died at Fredericksburg, Virginia, on October 1,
1978, eighteen days before he was to celebrate his ninety-
second birthday.

        The Rappahannock Industrial Academy did not close
without leaving an imprint on history, which is being perpetu-
ated through some of its graduates.   Among the distinguished
graduates of the Academy are: Luther Robinson, M. D. , Saint
Elizabeth's Hospital, Washington, D. C.; Lawrence Robinson,
Ph. D. (Harvard University), physiological chemist, Washing-
ton, D. C.; Julius Robinson, M. D. , Columbus, Ohio; George
Liverpool, retired principal, Maggie L. Walker High School,
Richmond; Booker T. Holmes, M. D. , Richmond; Randolph
White, mortician, Jamaica, Virginia; Ernest Gaines, business-
man, Tappahannock, Virginia; and the late Leslie Winston,
M. D. , of Richmond.

Pittsylvania Industrial, Normal, and Collegiate Institute, 1903-1934

When the Cherrystone Baptist Association agreed to accept the
proposal made by the Baptist General Association of Virginia
(Colored) to establish a school in Pittsylvania County, the illiteracy rate among the 21, 289 Black residents was very high.
The Danville Public High School for Blacks was available to
the 6, 515 Blacks who resided in that city, but education beyond
the elementary level was not available to the more than four-

teen thousand Black residents who lived in the rural areas of
the county.   The Cherrystone Baptist Association knew that
this situation existed and willingly accepted the suggestion by
the Baptist General Association (Colored) to do something
about it. The local Association decided to organize a school
at Gretna, and designate it the Pittsylvania Industrial, Normal, and Collegiate Institute.   The school was first organized
in the Elba Baptist Church in Gretna on March 16, 1903, by
Rev. G. W. Goode, with twenty-eight students.   Later in the
year, around October, the school was moved to a two-room
lodge hall, in which it remained until the Cherrystone Baptist
Association erected a school building on a forty-nine-acre
tract it purchased near Gretna.   In 1904, the Association
built a large two-story frame building on the property, which
contained several classrooms, offices, and boarding and lodging accommodations for girls. [110]

Dr. Goode served as an inspiration in the development
of the Institute.   A graduate of Virginia Union University and
pastor of the Calvary Baptist Church in Danville, he became
distinguished in Pittsylvania County as a minister-educator
prior to going to the Institute.   The local Association had
implicit faith in his ability to get the school started successfully. [111] Associated with him as pioneers in organizing the
school, raising funds, and recruiting students were W. F.
Grasty, M. L. Burton, both of Danville; Edward Lewis, S.
H. Dickerson, and Joseph Graves of Gretna; J. H. Fountain
of Keeling; W. B. Fitzgerald of Riceville; S. M. Taylor of
Ringo; and Rev. W. H. Carper of Chatham.

When Dr. Jesse Jones, Special Representative of the
United States Bureau of Education, visited the Institute in November 1914, three teachers were there who instructed thirty
elementary and fifteen secondary students.   Twenty-eight of
the students lived on the campus and were fed from produce
raised on the school's ten-acre farm.   By the end of the 1921
school year, there were more than one hundred students in attendance, one-half of whom were residents and three-fourths
in the secondary department. [112]

Rev. Goode remained Principal of the Institute until
1926, when he resigned due to poor health.   He was succeeded
by a former student, and the first graduate, Rev. R. J. Jones.
Jones, a graduate of Virginia Union University, was a resident
of Chatham.   He remained Principal of the Institute until 1955,
when the school was integrated. [113]

In 1934, during the administration of Rev. Jones, the Pittsylvania County Board of Education joined forces with the Cherrystone Baptist Association and the two exercised joint control over the Institute as a county high school for Blacks.[114]

For thirty-one years, from March 1903 to September 1934, the Cherrystone Baptist Association maintained the Pittsylvania Industrial, Normal, and Collegiate Institute under its control. The Baptist General Association of Virginia (Colored), the State Women's Missionary and Educational Convention, and the State Baptist Young People's Union each made a small donation to the local Association yearly for financial support of the school, but most of the financial support was furnished by the Black people of Pittsylvania County.

Among the teachers who served at the Institute were L. L. Tucker of Gretna, and R. B. Gaines, Marion Poole, I. W. Taylor, Rebecca Wright, Marie Taylor, and Rev. Chaffin of Danville. [115]

There were twenty-seven secondary-level graduating classes over the thirty-one years the school existed.   Each class averaged six graduates, for a total of approximately one hundred and sixty-two, who scattered throughout the county and engaged in various endeavors. [116]

Bowling Green Industrial Academy, 1903-1955

The history of the Bowling Green Industrial Academy is unique. In 1895, four years before the Baptist General Association of Virginia (Colored) was founded, the Caroline Baptist Sunday School Union initiated plans to establish a secondary-level school for the Black children of Caroline County. From that date until 1903, when the Bowling Green Industrial Academy was founded, the Union was busily engaged in raising money and purchasing property for the school.   It is acknowledged that the Baptist General Association of Virginia (Colored) had an impact on the founding of the Academy, through the contribution of two hundred dollars it donated to the Union for that purpose in 1902, but it is also acknowledged that the school would have been founded regardless.   The Black people of Caroline County were determined to do something to provide an adequate educational facility for their children.

In 1893, Rev. J. H. Turner, who was graduated from the Richmond Theological Seminary (Virginia Union University)

in 1890 and pastored the Shiloh Baptist Church in Bowling
Green, organized the Caroline Baptist Sunday School Union.
The purpose of the organization was to further the development
of the religious life of the Black people of Caroline County by
encouraging them to use Bibles in Sunday Schools.   Churches
that were charter members of the Union were: Shiloh Baptist
Church, Bowling Green; Jerusalem Baptist Church, Sparta; St.
Paul Baptist Church, Delos; and St. John Baptist Church, Milford.   Rev. Turner became the first President of the Union
and remained in the position until 1895 when he resigned to
accept a pastorate in another area. [117]

     When Turner left Caroline County, the work of the
Union had begun to lag.   There was only three dollars and
fifty-six cents in the Union's treasury, and the organization
was so loosely knit that it was on the verge of dissolution.
Concerned that the Union would disintegrate and the county
would be without a viable religious organization to reach all
of the Black people, several prominent Baptist leaders prevailed upon Rev. Randolph W. Young, pastor of the First
Mount Zion and Ebenezer Baptist Churches, Caroline County,
to become President.   Young, a very straightforward man,
told the committee that he would do so under one condition
only.   He asked that the Union membership cooperate with
him in undertaking to build and operate a boarding school to
furnish secondary education to the Black children of the county.
This was a serious proposition.   The Union was nearly defunct and any undertaking of that magnitude would certainly
require a great deal of money.   Nevertheless, the membership of the Union accepted the proposition and Young became
President of the organization in December 1895. [118]

     President Young and officers of the Union went to work
immediately building the organization to a position that it could
function with unity.   The membership had dropped from a high
of eight Sunday Schools in 1893 to three in 1895.   Over the
following six years, by 1901, it was increased to twelve Sunday Schools, all of which were committed to supporting Young's
plan for a school at Bowling Green.   In the meantime, the
Union had also increased its treasury, but not enough to purchase land on which to build a school.   The Union became interested in a tract of land, nineteen and three-quarter acres,
on the outskirts of Bowling Green, which was available for five
hundred dollars.   The treasury was growing, but the Union did
not have nearly enough money in 1901 to acquire the property.
Not willing to wait longer to get the school project started,
Rev. Young, with several of the Union officers, borrowed five

hundred dollars from a Mr. O. P. Smoot. They made themselves liable for the loan until such time as the Union would pay it off. [119]

After the land was purchased, the Union membership agreed to pay Smoot in full before attempting to borrow money to erect buildings. To this end, the Union staged a huge rally, in which it offered a special banner to the member church that raised the largest sum of money. The winning church was Shiloh Baptist of Bowling Green, which raised $215.92. The total effort resulted in the raising of enough money to pay the land note with a few dollars extra. The extra money was insufficient to execute the building plan in its entirety, but was enough to purchase materials with which to start erecting a frame building. Before purchasing any building materials, however, Rev. Young negotiated another loan to carry out the total building plan. [120]

In 1903, the first building was completed at the school site and designated Young Hall, in honor of the dedicated President of the Union, who was highly instrumental in making Bowling Green Industrial Academy a reality. The Building contained the girls' sleeping quarters, classrooms, and small chapel. [121]

Rev. Young was a thorough, persevering individual. He was not satisfied with simply building a secondary school; he also wanted to ensure that the students would receive a quality education within the school. Being familiar with Rev. L. L. Davis, a graduate of Hampton Institute and a prominent educator-religious leader of Essex County, Young asked him to become Principal of the Academy. Davis accepted and became the school's first Principal and vocational-agriculture teacher when it opened on October 4, 1903. There were five students enrolled in the first class. They were taught by Rev. Davis and one other teacher. [122]

The Bowling Green Industrial Academy was chartered in 1944 by the Virginia State Corporation Commission as a secondary school. Shortly thereafter, the Union appointed a Board of Trustees to manage the school, all of whom came from different churches of the organization. They were: R. B. Fortune, First Mount Zion Baptist Church, Caroline County; W. G. Young, Shiloh Baptist Church, Bowling Green; George Lonesome, Saint Paul Baptist Church, Delos; J. H. Bates, Mount Tabor Baptist Church, Caroline County; W. J. Young, Jerusalem Baptist Church, Sparta; T. M. Allen, Shiloh Baptist Church, Bowling Green; London Miles, Shiloh Baptist Church, Bowling Green; E. A. Johnson, Saint James Baptist

Church, Caroline County; and D. C. Winston, Mount Tabor Baptist Church, Caroline County. [123]

The Caroline Baptist Sunday School Union maintained the Bowling Green Industrial Academy as a secondary school for eleven years. During this time, the Union paid all expenses connected with the education of students who attended the school, to include instructional costs, upkeep of buildings and grounds, and boarding and lodging of students. Also, during the history of the Academy, the Union purchased an additional seven and three-quarter acres of land for school purposes. The money to purchase the land was raised by member churches of the Union and through a donation from a Frances E. Wright. [124]

In 1913, struggling to overcome the rising cost of living with corresponding increased operational costs, trustees of the Academy were forced to appeal to the County Superintendent of Schools, John Washington, for financial assistance. Washington referred the appeal to the Slater Fund, a philanthropic agency established in 1882 by John F. Slater of Connecticut for the purpose of helping to educate the emancipated population of the South. Assistance from the fund was forthcoming only if the county owned the school for which the money was intended. In 1914, in order to get financial assistance from the Slater Fund to keep the Academy open, the Union had to deed ten acres of its land, which contained all of the school buildings, to the Caroline County School Board.

When the Caroline County School Board gained control of the Academy, the school was redesignated the Caroline Training School and assigned a new Principal, Rev. G. Hayes Buchanan. Rev. Davis was appointed as the school's agriculture teacher. [125]

The transition brought to an end the Union's ownership of the Academy, but not its responsibility for operating and supporting the Caroline Training School. When the school opened in October 1914, the county furnished teachers and maintenance support, while the Union furnished the major support of the fuel and operated the boarding and lodging activities exclusively. [126]

During Buchanan's administration, in 1915, the enrollment at Caroline Training School reached two hundred and twelve students, only four of whom were boarders. To assist Buchanan were three teachers, all females. [127]

In 1920, due to an upsurge in the enrollment at the school, the Union erected another large frame building on the

campus.   It was paid for through funds raised by the Union,
donations from the Rosenwald Fund, and money bequeathed to
the school by Miss Frances E. Wright.   Members of the
Union, male and female, professional and lay, worked side
by side to construct the building.   Even the new Principal,
A. M. Walker, who succeeded Buchanan in 1919, worked
evenings and Sundays to help complete the building. [128]

By 1926, the Caroline Training School had grown to the
extent that the Union decided it was necessary to build a new
auditorium to replace the original, which was built in 1903.
The President of the Union, H. P. Latney, assisted by the
Principal, Rev. H. M. Ruffin, who succeeded Mr. Walker in
1925, raised two hundred dollars and secured one hundred
dollars from the Caroline County School Board for the project.
With other funds raised by individuals and organizations, the
Union built the auditorium.   When the building effort was completed, in the summer of 1926, Rev. Ruffin resigned as Principal.   In October 1926, he was replaced by Rev. Hovey Rice
Young, a graduate of Virginia Union University.   His first official act was to notify both the Caroline County School Board
and Caroline Baptist Sunday School Union that he was going to
do everything in his power to get the school accredited by the
state.   After two years of hard work, in 1928, he accomplished
his goal when the school received accreditation by the state of
Virginia as a four-year high school. [129]

After Caroline Training School was accredited, the
Principal, Union officials, and the Caroline County School
Board agreed that the name of the school should be changed
to one more appropriate to the accreditation.   At the suggestion of a faculty member, Gertrude Young, wife of Rev. A.
P. Young, pastor of Shiloh Baptist Church in Bowling Green,
and a teacher in the Caroline Training School, the school was
redesignated Union High School.   Mrs. Young suggested the name
in commemoration of the Caroline Baptist Sunday School Union. [130]

In 1940, George B. Ruffin, brother of H. M. Ruffin,
became Principal of Union High School.   During his administration, 1940-69, the school grew to become twice as large
as the white high school at Bowling Green.   It had such a
diversified curriculum that after schools were integrated, most
of the county students clamored to go there.   It became so
popular that it was finally redesignated Bowling Green High
School, in 1969. [131]

The Caroline Baptist Sunday School Union rendered financial support to Union High School until 1955, when the

county school system was integrated.   At that time, the county took over full support of the school.   For the first time in fifty-two years, the Caroline Baptist Sunday School Union was out of the business of educating Blacks in Caroline County at the secondary level.   The Union then concentrated its efforts on intensifying Bible study in the county and supporting Virginia Union University, Virginia Seminary, and foreign missions. [132]

Holmes School (King William Academy; Hamilton-Holmes High School), 1903-1955

United States Bureau of the Census statistics indicate that 4,962 Blacks, nearly 60 percent of the total county population, resided in King William County in 1900.   The illiteracy rate among Blacks was 25 percent for those who were ten years of age and over.   There was need for improvement in the public elementary school facilities and to provide the Black population with a secondary school at which teachers could be prepared to instruct other Blacks. [133]

Rev. Samuel B. Holmes, head teacher at Ruffin Academy, Cauthornsville, King and Queen County, pastored a Baptist church in King William County and was familiar with the educational status of Blacks there.   Many members of the church he pastored were illiterate.   Most of them clamored for an education, but due to the lack of educational facilities in the county, they were not able to attend school.   It was nearly impossible for the majority of them to attend the several sparsely located elementary schools.   Holmes was highly displeased with the appalling educational dilemma Blacks confronted in King William County, and resolved to remedy the condition to the best of his ability.   His first move was to open a combination elementary-secondary school in a one-room log cabin near King William Court House, in late November 1903.   It was not initially intended as a boarding school, but several students from distant areas, resided with members of the community the first year.   The school was named the Holmes School after its founder. [134]

Due to yearly increases in enrollment, Rev. Holmes was forced periodically to move his school to larger log cabins. Finally, in 1908, he purchased several acres of land near King William Court House and constructed a large frame building, which contained one office and several classrooms.   In the same year, the Pamunkey Baptist Association, which served

King William and King and Queen Counties, became financially involved with the school through lending Rev. Holmes money with which to complete the building project. In that the sum given to the school was considerably more than Rev. Holmes had invested, the Association assumed operational control of the school and renamed it King William Academy. From 1908 to 1923, the Pamunkey Baptist Association was the primary source of income for the Academy. In 1923, the school was taken over by the King William County Board of Education and redesignated the Hamilton-Holmes High School in honor of Samuel B. Holmes, the founder, and a Mr. Hamilton, a prominent Black resident of the county who supported the school financially during its initial years. [135]

The Hamilton-Holmes High School remained an all-Black institution after the county took control of it. Nevertheless, the Pamunkey Baptist Association continued to support the school through providing funds for special activities, office furnishings, athletic equipment, library books, and other materials and equipment. It was not until 1955, when the school was integrated, that the Pamunkey Baptist Association stopped supporting Hamilton-Holmes High School, after fifty-two years. [136]

Rev. Holmes did not demand more from his students than he was willing to give of himself. While serving as Principal of the King William Academy, he attended Virginia Union University during the summer months until 1922, when he was graduated with the Bachelor of Divinity degree. The following year, he was awarded the honorary Doctor of Divinity degree by Virginia Union University in recognition of the excellent work he had done in King William County. [137]

Fredericksburg Normal and Industrial Institute
(Mayfield High School), 1905-1938

Historic Fredericksburg, Spotsylvania County, nestled in the valley on the banks of the Rappahannock River, is situated midway between Richmond and Washington, D. C. In 1900, the city had a Black population of 1,621, or 32 percent of the total population. Among those in the Black population who were ten years of age and over, there was a literacy rate of 80 percent. The city was indeed fortunate to have had such a high literacy rate, but could claim only a small amount of credit for the accomplishment. It was due primarily to the pervasive attitude concerning the extreme value of education

that was held in the Black community.   Due to their persistence
over the years, the city had provided them with an elementary
school in the last quarter of the nineteenth century, long before Virginia cities of comparable size did the same for their
Black residents.   The Black community did not, however, fare
as well in regard to getting a secondary educational facility in
Fredericksburg.   Their pleas were ignored on that subject,
and this incensed the Black leaders to the point they decided
to establish their own.

In the early spring of 1905, Rev. James E. Brown,
pastor of Shiloh Old Site Baptist Church in Fredericksburg,
received a letter from Rev. J. H. Pressley, pastor of a Baptist church at Orange, which asked him to send a committee
to Orange Court House to discuss founding a regional secondary school for Blacks.   At a meeting in the Shiloh Old Site
Baptist Church, called by Brown and composed of Black civic
and educational leaders, a committee was named to attend the
meeting.   Members of the committee were: J. E. Brown,
chairman; Rev. Samuel A. Brown, Principal of the Fredericksburg Public School for Blacks and pastor of the Mount Hope
Baptist Church in Brooke; and S. G. Willis, deacon of Shiloh
New Site Baptist Church in Fredericksburg.   The three men
had been at the forefront for civil rights in Fredericksburg
for many years.   They led the fight initially to get the city
to provide a secondary school for its Black citizens, as it had
done for the white citizens.   Their instructions from their
peers were to prevail upon those in attendance at the Orange
Court House meeting that the school had to be located at Fredericksburg.   When the meeting was convened at Orange Court
House, there were several communities represented, each with
instructions to bring the school to its area.   There was so
much bickering over where the school should be located that
the meeting proved to be a failure as far as founding a regional secondary school; it did, however, serve to inspire the
Black people of Fredericksburg to come together and establish
a secondary school on their own. [138]

In early September 1905, through the efforts of Samuel
A. Brown, a group of about fifteen citizens met at the home
of Joseph Walker to discuss final plans to open a secondary
school.   A Board of Trustees was elected for the school, with
Samuel Brown serving as president; Jason Grant, secretary;
and Joseph Walker, chairman.   Grant, also a prominent civic
leader, was a teacher in the public school for Blacks.   Walker was a deacon at Shiloh New Site Baptist Church, Fredericksburg, and prominent civil-rights leader.   Each person at the

meeting pledged ten dollars toward getting the school opened
the following month, in October.   The school was named the
Fredericksburg Normal and Industrial Institute, and P. C.
Whitely, a graduate of Virginia Union University who was
present at the meeting at the request of Samuel Brown, was
appointed Principal. [139]

On October 2, 1905, the Institute opened to students in
the basement of the Shiloh New Site Baptist Church, which had
been rented by the Board of Trustees.   The school consisted
of P. C. Whitely, teacher-principal, and between ten and fifteen students.   During its first year, the Institute was a huge
success, due largely to the support given by the Black baptists
of Fredericksburg, and the membership of the Mt. Hope Baptist Church in Brooke.   It was so successful that the Board
of Trustees found it expedient to purchase quickly a permanent
site for the school.   The President of the Institute, Samuel
Brown, was chosen by the Board to find a site and report to
it what had been found. [140]

Through the cooperation of Joseph Walker, Chairman
of the Board of Trustees and sexton of the historic St. George's
Episcopal Church, Fredericksburg, and Judge A. T. Embrey,
for whom Walker once worked and by whom he was highly respected, Brown found Howison Farm, several miles south of
Fredericksburg.   The farm, known as "Moorefield," had formerly been owned by the late Mr. Owens of the Owens and
Minor Drug Company in Richmond.   The property was then,
in 1906, in the hands of the Virginia Trust Company, which
was represented by Judge Embrey.   It consisted of fifty-five
acres of farm land with a large farmhouse, valued at twelve
hundred dollars.   After it was shown to the Board of Trustees
and they gave approval to acquire it, the site was purchased.
Shortly thereafter, Judge Embrey suggested that the name
"Moorefield" should be replaced with a better sounding name
for a school, as "Mayfield."   His suggestion was accepted by
the Board and the name of the school was redesignated Mayfield High School.   Notwithstanding the name change, through
the years both Fredericksburg Normal and Industrial Institute
and Mayfield High School have been used interchangeably in
referring to the school. [141]

The large farmhouse that was situated on the Mayfield
High School site contained a large kitchen, with seven living
and bedrooms on the first and second floors.   Although the
house was in need of minor repairs, it was an excellent building for a boarding-school facility.   After it was repaired and

slightly renovated, the school was relocated to the new location in the fall of 1906. Rev. Samuel Brown, President, and his wife, Clementine, moved in and took charge of the school's boarding department. Two rooms on the first floor were used as classrooms and the others were available for female resident students and the President's family. Later around 1908, two large rooms were added for classroom space. Around 1914, a building was constructed that contained three spacious sleeping rooms for boys and one large classroom. The sleeping room accommodated twelve boys each. Until the building was constructed, boys who attended Mayfield High School resided with families in the vicinity of school. [142]

The first administration of Mayfield High School was that of Rev. Brown. He served as the nonteaching President, assisted by the teacher-principal P. C. Whitely, and Mr. J. William Moss. In 1907, during the latter half of the second year of its history at Mayfield, the board of trustees employed Rev. W. L. Ransome, pastor of the Shiloh New Site Baptist Church, as an assistant teacher. Ransome, a graduate of Virginia Union University, was eager to impart knowledge to the children of Fredericksburg. He had expressed his willingness to help foster the growth of the school in any way that he could. [143]

The second Principal of Mayfield High School was J. W. Moss. Moss, a graduate of the College Department, Virginia Normal Institute in Petersburg, replaced Whitely in 1907. He resigned in 1909 and relocated to West Virginia. Moss was succeeded as Principal by W. L. Ransome. Ransome held the position until 1913, when he was elevated to the position of President-Principal. He held both positions until 1920, when he resigned to accept the pastorate of the First Baptist Church in South Richmond. [144]

When Ransome became President-Principal of Mayfield High School, the school's existence was threatened by lack of funds. He was successful in overcoming this obstacle by obtaining funds from several sources that had been previously untapped: the Women's Missionary and Educational Convention, the Baptist State Sunday School Convention, and the Baptist General Association (Colored). He was also instrumental in obtaining a small amount of financial support from the City of Fredericksburg. Serving as spokesman for a committee that appeared before the Fredericksburg City Council in 1914 to seek financial assistance for the high school, Ransome presented his case with such eloquence that the council voted unanimously to give the school two hundred dollars annually. Before he left the city, in 1920, he made many more appearances before the council appealing for funds and was successful. The annual city appropriation rose from two hundred dollars to eighteen hundred dollars by 1920. Even though the entire Board of Trustees consisted of Baptists and some financial assistance was received from three Baptist organizations, Mayfield High School was maintained on an independent basis throughout its history. The only agreement it had with any group in exchange for financial support was with the city of Fredericksburg--not to charge city students tuition. Neither the city of Fredericksburg nor the Baptist General Association of Virginia (Colored) exercised control over the school.[145]

Mayfield High School was accredited by the Virginia State Board of Education during Ransome's administration. Graduates thereafter for many years were given a professional certificate to teach in the elementary schools of Virginia for one year.

The third administration at Mayfield High School was that of Rev. John A. Bacoates, who joined the faculty under the presidency of Ransome. Bacoates expanded the physical plant through adding a large new building with four spacious classrooms, a science laboratory, and twenty rooms for resident students. Funds for the project came largely from the Board of Trustees; city churches; Mt. Hope Baptist Church in Brooke; and Jason C. Grant, Secretary of the Mayfield High School. The building project climaxed Bacoates's short tenure as President-Principal. He left the school around 1925 to assume the presidency of Leland College in Louisiana. [146]

The next administration was that of Rev. B. H. Hester, pastor of Shiloh Old Site Baptist Church in Fredericksburg, who was elected President-Principal in 1926. Rev. Melvin L. Murchison, pastor of Shiloh New Site Baptist Church, also in Fredericksburg, was appointed Business Manager and Treasurer of the school at the same time. The two men worked together and paid all of the debts of the school, increased its enrollment, and brought the school to a level where it was once again accredited by the Virginia State Board of Education, which had dropped it during Bacoates's administration. [147]

By 1935, the Board of Trustees of Mayfield High School and Black citizens of Fredericksburg began to communicate their feelings to the city on having carried the major burden of providing the Black youths of Fredericksburg with a secondary educational facility for thirty years. Having discharged what they termed a "city responsibility" for all of those years, they made it clear that they were no longer willing to carry on in the future as they had done in the past. Financial aid from the several state Baptist organizations was almost nill, and yet the school enrollment increased greatly each year. It was only through the financial genius of the Business Manager, Melvin Murchison, and the superb management by the matron, Naomi S. Dabney, that the Hester administration survived to 1935. The work of the Hester-Murchison-Dabney team deserves great credit. Had it not been for that team's managerial ability, the school would likely have failed. Even so, when the team was broken up in 1935, the school suffered a tremendous loss. [148]

The fourth administration was that of George L. Vick, who succeeded B. H. Hester in 1935. Vick remained at the school for one academic year and left to attend dental school. [149]

The last administration was that of Paul E. Bowes, who served as Principal from September 1936 through June 1938. Bowes was also a strong advocate of the city taking over responsibility for educating its Black youths at the secondary level. Within a few months after he became Principal of Mayfield High School, he made a strong, urgent appeal to the enlightened white citizenry of the city to support the cause to have the city of Fredericksburg assume its responsibility to its Black citizens through providing a public-supported secondary school for their children. [150]

After repeated requests from the Black citizens over many years, the city of Fredericksburg acquiesced in 1938 by building a twenty-five-thousand-dollar secondary-level addition to the new elementary school it had built in 1935. The construction was completed, and the public high school was opened on November 1, 1938. The new public-supported high school brought to an end the Black Baptist-supported Mayfield High School, which had been in continuous operation for thirty-three years.

In the final year Mayfield High School was open, 1937-38, it had a faculty of five and one matron, all of whom possessed baccalaureate degrees. Three courses of study were offered students for graduation. They were the Academic course, which consisted of four units of English, three of

Mathematics, two of Science, and five electives, for a total
of sixteen; the Vocational course, which consisted of four units
of English, one of Business, four of Home Economics, two of
History, two of Science, and four electives, for a total of
eighteen; and the Industrial course (Masonry), which consisted
of four units of Practical Mechanics, two of Mechanical Draw-
ing, four of English, three of Mathematics, one-half unit of
Industrial Hygiene, one-half of Industrial History, two units of
History and Business, and two of Science, for a total of eighteen units. [151]

In 1938, students at Mayfield High School were evalu-
ated on the following basis:

Table 4

MAYFIELD HIGH SCHOOL GRADING SYSTEM, 1938

Grade	Grade Points
A: 95-100	4
B: 88-94	3
C: 81-87	2
D: 75-80	1
F: Below 75-Failing	---

From its inception, Mayfield High School was a reli-
gious-oriented institution. The leadership believed firmly that
religion was fundamental to human advancement, and students
were to be given every opportunity to develop their moral and
spiritual lives. In an effort to promote this strong belief,
school administrators were mandated to program religious services on a regular basis. Hence, principals required teachers
to conduct devotional services daily at the beginning of their
classes for years. The matron, assisted by one of the faculty
members, conducted prayer services twice weekly, the attendance at which was required of resident students. Church services were held once during the week, usually on Fridays.
Sundays were set aside for students to attend one of the local
churches, if the student did not go home for the weekend.
For the purpose of giving even greater stimulation to spiritual
life, an annual week of prayer was conducted each spring,
which all students were required to attend. [152]

Organizations constituted an important influence on the cultural and intellectual development of Mayfield High School students. The more significant student clubs and societies were: the Honorary Society, which was composed of students who maintained a 2.6 average, and above; the Dunbar Literary Society, which met weekly and featured literary achievements among students and guests; the Choral Club, which was composed of a select group of young men and women; the Dramatic Club, which usually presented a series of plays during the academic year; and the Debating Society, which on several occasions took part in the Virginia State Championship Debates. Two important social clubs were "Rendezvous" and "The Ducky Wucky Club."[153]

Major sports were encouraged for the purpose of moral and physical development. Contests in baseball, basketball, football, and tract were held with other schools in northern Virginia.

Some of the more prominent graduates of Mayfield High School are: Jason C. Grant, Jr., retired professor of English, and Carolyn Grant, retired professor of music, both of Howard University; Dr. Douglas Bowes, dentist; Mary Bowes, a graduate of Howard University; Nannie Bowes Norbrey, a graduate of Howard University and retired instructor of romance languages in the city of Fredericksburg; Paul E. Bowes, a graduate of Howard University and retired Principal of James Lee School, Newport News, Virginia; Dr. Maurice Tate, pharmacist, Fredericksburg; Maurice Norbrey, a graduate of Virginia Union University, and United States Correction Officer, Petersburg; Bessie Tate Proctor, a graduate of Virginia Union University, and wife of Dr. Samual DeWitt Proctor, Pastor of Abyssinia Baptist Church, New York City; Grant Wright, retired chief of the Park Police Service, Washington, D.C.; and Naomi Brooks Wright, educator, Howard University.

The late Dr. W. L. Ransome asserted that as far as he was concerned, "the Fredericksburg Normal and Industrial Institute was the best Negro Church school" he had known.[154] It is indeed a fitting and justly deserved tribute to an outstanding school.

Three of the more influential Black leaders at the forefront for secondary education in 1905 were Jason C. Grant, Joseph Walker, and Frederick D. Bowes. Grant was for many years a teacher in the Fredericksburg Public School for Blacks. He was always a strong critic of the city administration for failing to provide a secondary educational facility for Black youths. Walker supported Grant's stand and worked alongside his friend for the cause for many years. Bowes, a United States Government postal employee and a compeer of Grant and Walker, also gave strong support to the effort. Had it not been for the perseverance of these three men, before and after Fredericksburg Normal and Industrial Institute was founded, it is likely that there would not have been support from the city of Fredericksburg for Mayfield High School or a public-supported high school, even as early as 1938. [155]

Nansemond Collegiate Institute (Nansemond Institute), 1905-1935

Nansemond County had a Black population of 12,962 in 1900, or 56 percent of the total county population. More than twenty-five hundred of the Black population lived in the only city in the county, Suffolk. Seven hundred of the Black residents of Suffolk attended the one public elementary school that was available for them. In the rural areas, there were only a few public elementary schools for the Black population. Throughout the county, educational facilities for Blacks were inadequate, and the county did practically nothing to change the condition. This was appalling, as the illiteracy rate among Blacks who were ten years of age and over was 35 percent and rising. Not one secondary-level educational facility was available to Black residents in the entire county, public or private. There was no opportunity for Black residents of the county to obtain a high school education without traveling to another county. [156]

Rev. William H. Gaines, a graduate of Wayland Seminary, Washington, D. C., and pastor of the First Baptist Church in Suffolk, became increasingly incensed over the years of his pastorate with the poor treatment Blacks received in education at Nansemond County, and constantly fought for change. From the time he became pastor of the First Baptist Church, in 1889, until 1905, when he organized the first combination elementary-secondary school in the county, he prodded county authorities to provide adequate educational service to its citizens. His pleas were unheeded for so many years that finally he called the Black citizens together and prevailed upon them to join him in founding and supporting a school.

With the assistance of many Black citizens of Nansemond

County and the Sharon Baptist Association (an affiliate of the
Virginia Baptist State Convention), he rented an old farm on
the outskirts of Suffolk for the purpose of opening a school.
The farm, which consisted of thirty-nine acres, was known
as the Lloyd residence. It was converted to a school by Gaines
and other community members through funds received from
the Sharon Baptist Association. The Association designated
the school Nansemond Collegiate Institute and hired Rev. William
H. Morris of Rich Square, North Carolina, as its Principal.

On or about October 5, 1905, the Nansemond Collegiate
Institute opened to students from the county. The initial enrollment consisted of approximately twenty students, the majority of whom were from Suffolk. There was no boarding
department attached to the school. Students who came from
areas beyond Suffolk were given accommodations with Suffolk
residents who lived within walking distance of the Institute.
The school operated on that basis until 1909, when the Sharon
Baptist Association purchased the Lloyd farm and erected a
large three-story building that contained sixteen rooms. Several rooms, on the first and second floors, were set aside as
classrooms, while the third floor was used as a boys' residence area. In 1910, another building was erected to accommodate female students in residence. [157]

Rev. James Albert Harrell, a native of Corapeake,
North Carolina, became the second Principal of the Institute.
He succeeded Morris in 1913, two years after he had suc-
ceeded Gaines as pastor of the First Baptist Church, Suffolk.
Harrell was a graduate of the high school department at the
Saint Paul Normal and Industrial Institute, Lawrenceville, Vir-
ginia, and the Theology Department, Virginia Union University,
Richmond, in 1904. [158]

Unfortunately, Harrell's administration was plagued with
many problems, and the Institute suffered severely. Harrell
was so oriented toward industrial education that the academic
curriculum was woefully neglected. When representatives of
the United States Bureau of Education, led by Dr. Jesse Jones,
visited the institution on April 1, 1915, the comment was made
that "the instruction was unsuited to the needs of the pupils."
It was recommended by the evaluators that the school be made
a county training school. Although he tried very hard to improve the image of the Institute and move it forward over the
next two years, Harrell was unable to do so. Finally, in
1917, he resigned the principalship of Nansemond Collegiate
Institute and devoted full time to his ministerial duties. [159]

The third Principal of the Institute was a Mr. Bruce,
who succeeded Harrell on or about October 1, 1917. Under
Bruce's leadership, the school expanded its operation and
opened an industrial department, which contained a large printing press that eventually became the central printing source
for Nansemond County. It was also during Bruce's administration that Suffolk's first Black newspaper, The Dismal Swamp
Echo was published, under the direct supervision of the head
of the Industrial Department of the Institute. After serving as
Principal for two academic years, Bruce resigned in 1919.
He was succeeded by Rev. Thomas J. Johnson, a graduate of
Virginia Union University. 160

Johnson, assisted by his wife, did an outstanding job
of raising Nansemond Collegiate Institute to a higher plateau.
The two formed a formidable team that worked in unison to
bring the school to a state where it once again enjoyed a good
reputation. They organized Choral and Dramatic Clubs that
won acclaim throughout the state of Virginia and brought a
wealth of publicity to the school. The printing-press operation also became a source of deep interest in the entire county,
as residents went to the school in large numbers to have
printing done. The Johnsons kept up the good work at the
school until 1925, when Rev. Johnson resigned to accept a
position elsewhere. 161

The fifth Principal, Rev. John M. Henderson, was a
1924 graduate of the Theology Department, Virginia Union University. He replaced Johnson in September 1925 and remained
at the school through May 1926, when he was succeeded by
William A. Huskerson, a civil engineer. Huskerson's assumption of duty as Principal was very timely. The Board of
Trustees of Nansemond Collegiate Institute was in the process
of expanding the school's physical plant and had need for some-
one with a background in engineering. The Board had borrowed fifteen thousand dollars from several local banks for
the purpose of erecting a building, and wanted to be certain
that it got the most for its money. The building plans were
given to Huskerson and he was asked to build it. The proposed structure, a large, modern brick building, was designed
to replace the three-story frame building, which had been
erected in 1910 under the leadership of the first Principal,
William H. Morris.

Huskerson completed the building project in early 1928.
Shortly thereafter, the Board of Trustees changed the name of
the school to Nansemond Institute. In late 1928, Nansemond

Institute was accredited by the Virginia State Board of Education and became the first secondary school to be accredited in Suffolk.   Students at the Nansemond County Training School for Blacks, which was built in 1919, had to spend two years at Nansemond Institute to prepare themselves for acceptance in college. [162]

During the early 1930s, Nansemond Institute began to suffer the acute pains of the Depression.   Many of the local Baptist churches, which had given the school financial support for over a quarter of a century, were no longer able to do so.   Parents who sent their children there, despite the availability of a county training school, could no longer afford to do so.   The school began to suffer a serious decline in enrollment and deterioration in the physical plant.   A final injury, in 1934 the brick building, which was constructed by Huskerson in 1928, burned beyond repair.   Huskerson, in a last effort to keep the school open, quickly opened other buildings to classes, but this did not work.   Finally, in 1935, due to circumstances beyond the control of the school authorities, and many interested others, the school was closed permanently. [163]

There are many outstanding graduates of Nansemond Collegiate Institute (Nansemond Institute).   Among them are: Judge Herbert Benn, retired; Rev. Fred Vann, pastor, First Baptist Church; and Mr. Sidney Estes, prominent fraternal leader and construction engineer--all of Suffolk; Dr. W. P. Richardson, dentist, Franklin, Virginia; and Henry Bass, scientist, New York State. [164]

Corey Memorial Institute (Smallwood-Corey Industrial and Collegiate Institute), 1906-1928

Corey Memorial Institute was founded at Portsmouth, Norfolk County, in 1906, by the Norfolk Union Baptist Association, an affiliate of the Baptist General Association of Virginia (Colored). It was named in honor of the late Dr. Charles H. Corey, who was at one time President of Richmond Theological Seminary (Virginia Union University).   The Institute, a large three-story frame building, was built on eight city lots and contained an office, several classrooms, and boarding and lodging facilities.

The first Principal of the Institute was Rev. Benjamin E. McWilliams, a native of Toledo, Ohio, and a graduate of Virginia Union University, Richmond.   He organized the school single-handedly during its initial years, serving as both teacher and Principal until he resigned in 1912 to accept a pastorate elsewhere. He was succeeded by Rev. J. Early Wright, also a graduate of Virginia Union University. Wright remained at the Institute until 1915, when he was succeeded by Rev. Charles H. Morton, a native of Staunton, Virginia, and a graduate of Lincoln University, Oxford, Pennsylvania. Morton went to Corey Memorial Institute from Mathews County, Virginia, where he had pastored the Ebenezer and Antioch Baptist Churches for three years. His previous educational experience was that of teaching Science, English, and Latin at Spiller Academy in Hampton, in 1897. He was a strong advocate of education and held the belief that it is through education that the Black race will eventually elevate itself to a level of acceptance in society. [165] In 1918, Morton was succeeded by Rev. H. M. Henderson of Suffolk, Virginia, who became the fourth administrator of the Institute.

By 1919, under Henderson's principalship, the enrollment at Corey Memorial Institute reached a point beyond which the school was not physically able to accommodate more students. The Norfolk Union Baptist Association became concerned about the matter and prevailed upon the Baptist General Association to render assistance in resolving the matter. In early 1920, the Baptist General Association purchased a hundred-and-seventy-two-acre tract of land at Claremont. The site, which had been previously occupied by Smallwood Memorial Institute, a private, nondenominational elementary school, contained nine large buildings that were ideally suited to the needs of Corey Memorial Institute. The property also consisted of a large pier that was on the site where the second cargo of Black slaves landed in America in the seventeenth century. The total value of the property was estimated to be more than a quarter of a million dollars in 1920. [166]

Smallwood Memorial Institute had been owned and operated by Rev. John J. Smallwood, Ph. D. , from 1894 to 1911. In 1913, the Chancery Court of Surry County placed the property in the hands of receivers to sell it to satisfy the indebtedness. The Baptist General Association of Virginia (Colored) purchased the property in 1920. [167]

In May 1921, Corey Memorial Institute was moved to Claremont and renamed the Smallwood-Corey Memorial Industrial and Collegiate Institute, according to the charter recorded at the Surry Court House. The same document states that the curriculum would include in addition to the ordinary branches of education, instruction in Industrial Arts, Agriculture, Classical Education, and Theology. [168]

Rev. Robert J. Langston was appointed Principal of Smallwood-Corey Industrial and Collegiate Institute in 1921. He succeeded Henderson and opened the school at Claremont. Langston was a graduate of Virginia Union University and had been pastor of the Bank Street Baptist Church in Norfolk. He became the fifth administrator of the school. During his tenure, 1921-1924, the Institute experienced a significant increase in enrollment. Within one academic year, by September 1922, the enrollment was one hundred students. This was the largest enrollment in the history of the school to that date. Under his leadership, the faculty was also increased. It rose to nine, the largest number in the history of the school. Further, a larger percentage of the student body were resident students than at any prior time. [169]

In 1924, the Baptist General Association reappointed H. M. Henderson as Principal to succeed Langston, who retired. Henderson remained Principal through May 1926, when he resigned. The school suffered severe financial difficulty during the same year, which caused the Board of Trustees to reach out for help. Contact was made with the Marcus Garvey movement, which stressed a back-to-Africa theme, and some understanding was reached to keep the school open. From September 1926 through June 1928, the Institute was subsidized by both the Universal Negro Improvement Association (Marcus Garvey's organization) and the Baptist General Association of Virginia (Colored). Caleb Robinson, Claremont, was the school's seventh and final administrator. When the school session concluded in June 1928, Robinson, accompanied by the faculty and student body, departed the school and did not return. Within a short period, the school was vandalized and rendered unsuitable for further habitation. For the next thirteen years the property remained under control of the Board of Trustees; in June 1941, it was sold. [170]

V. SUMMARY

During the time of slavery, from 1619 until 1861, it was generally held a crime, in those states in which slaveholding was legal, to teach Blacks to read and write. However, in Virginia many Blacks learned both skills through the kindness of their masters, who either taught them or arranged for them to be taught.

In the main, the restriction against the education of Virginia Blacks was accomplished through acts of legislation. For example, Virginia in 1819 forbade

... all meetings or assemblages of slaves or free negroes or mulattoes, mixing or associating with such slaves ... at any school or schools for teaching them reading or writing either in the day or night. [1]

In late 1831, after the Nat Turner Insurrection at Southampton County, Virginia, on August 21, 1831, another law was enacted that provided that

... all meetings of negroes or mulattoes, at any school house, or other place for teaching them reading and writing, either in the day or night, under whatever pretext, shall be deemed and considered an unlawful assembly. [2]

Though many thousands of Blacks learned to read and write during the course of slavery, in 1860 more than 90 percent of the Black population of Virginia--490,865--were illiterate. [3]

The meager, mainly informal, and often clandestine and unlawful instruction the slaves received did not prepare

104

them for participation in a free society.   However, during the
Civil War, and the Reconstruction period that followed, ex-
slaves witnessed the advent of a new era of educational opportunity.

        The new era began in September 1861, at Fortress
Monroe, Virginia, when Rev. Lewis C. Lockwood of the
American Missionary Association, began a school program
for Black refugees.   Within a three-day period, he opened a
Sunday School and then a day school for Blacks.   When Lockwood left Fortress Monroe thirteen months later, day and
night schools operated with an enrollment of seven thousand
students and Sunday Bible classes of five thousand.

        The educational work of the American Missionary As-
sociation was exemplary.   After the Civil War, it was followed
by many other denominational groups, such as the American
Baptist Home Mission Society, the Methodists, the Catholics,
and the Black Baptist Churches, among other missionary and
philanthropic groups.   The work of these organizations was
fruitful at the elementary level, but handicapped due to the
widespread indifference to the education of Blacks at the secondary and higher levels.   This was a great injustice heaped
on the children of the Black race.   They were denied opportunity to receive the cultural training that accompanied higher
education, and the incentive to perseverance, which is important to children in adolescence.   Moreover, contrary to the
popular belief among white Virginians that Blacks paid no taxes
and should not be educated at public expense, many Blacks
were large property owners.   They paid a large share of
taxes, for which they received no educational benefit.   Finally,
Virginia did little more after the Civil War to promote the
education of the Black race than it did during the antebellum
period.   The state was, in fact, woefully negligent in the discharge of its moral obligation to take action to provide adequately for the education of Black inhabitants.   Blinded by her
obsession to keep the Black race in ignorance, Virginia failed
to realize that the sum total of her intelligence, culture, and
refinement was far less than it would have been had she provided public high schools for Blacks on a larger scale.   Even
though the state organized its public school system in 1870,
there were only four public-supported high schools for the
671,096 Black inhabitants in 1910. [4]

        The foundation of the education of the Black race in
Virginia was the church.   From 1619, when the first twenty
indentured slaves landed at Jamestown, to the present, the

church has played a most significant role in the education of
Blacks in Virginia.   During slavery, church missionaries went
throughout the Colony, when allowed, teaching religious subjects to Christianize the poor wretched slaves.   From this
relationship, the Black church evolved.   From history, we
learned that the early Black church existed as the arena out
of which all issues relating to Black life and existence could
be addressed.   It served as a social hall where Black people
could share fellowship and talent.   Out of paltry resources,
the Black church struggled to build educational institutions at
all levels.   It also gave birth to the Black preacher, the most
influential individual in the Black community.   Historically,
the Black minister served the Black community as preacher,
teacher, psychiatrist, family counselor, community organizer,
lawyer, judge, and jury.

Black Baptist preachers, many of whom were trained,
after the Civil War, through schools supported by the American Baptist Home Mission Society, were among the first persons to recognize the seriousness of the educational situation
in Virginia as it affected the Black race.   Many of the preachers were born in slavery and had lived through trials and trib-
ulations in regard to their own education as well as that of
their fellows.   Based on their experiences, they had little faith
that the state of Virginia would do anything to support the education of Blacks beyond the trifling little it was doing; therefore, they initiated action to remedy the problem as it per-
tained to providing secondary education to Black Virginians.
The contributions of these preachers included both establishing
and supporting secondary schools throughout the state.   On
many occasions, they founded schools and also became teachers
and principals within the school.   They were determined to
make democracy work by proving to their state and nation that
the Black race was a responsible entity that desired to share
the American dream.

Had the education of the freedmen of Virginia been left
wholly to the state of Virginia, it seems certain that Black
Virginians would even today be victimized by the great curse
of ignorance and its associated ills (disease, crime, economic
dependency) to a far greater extent than they are today.   Conditions paralleling those found in certain isolated areas of
Mississippi, Alabama, and certain other southern states might
well be found characteristic of Virginia had it not been for the
decisive action taken by so many Christian men and women
after the Civil War.

During the period 1887 through 1957, there were thirteen secondary schools established and operated under the
control of Black Baptists in Virginia.   Several were established
and operated under the control of the district Baptist associations, the Virginia State Baptist Sunday School Convention, and
the Virginia State Women's Missionary and Educational Convention.   All of the privately owned Black Baptist secondary
schools were established to expand the educational opportunities for Black boys and girls to prepare themselves for greater
service to humanity.   Most were incorporated, and characterized by what Katz has described as the democratic-localism
mode of education.   The local Baptist associations prescribed
the curricula that were to be followed, without interference
from the state of Virginia, until the schools were accredited.
There were other Black Baptist-supported private secondary
schools that were characterized by what Katz described as the
corporate voluntarism-mode of education.   They were financed
through a combination of endowments and tuition fees.   The
Virginia Seminary, at Lynchburg, is an example of this model.
For several years, when it operated under the "Compact" arrangement with the American Baptist Home Mission Society,
it was endowed by that organization.   Support for the school
then came from tuition, the Virginia Baptist State Convention,
and the endowment from the American Baptist Home Mission
Society.   There were also those schools that ultimately came
under city and county supervision and assumed what Katz has
described as the incipient-bureaucracy mode of education.
The city and county boards of education exercised control over
their curricula and mandated that children were to attend
school through a certain age.   The Bowling Green Industrial
Academy and Mayfield High School are examples of the incipient-bureaucracy mode. [5]

There are two privately owned Black Baptist institutions
of higher learning currently operating in the state of Virginia.
They are Virginia Union University, which was founded at
Richmond in 1865 by the American Baptist Home Mission Society, and Virginia College (Virginia Seminary), which was
founded at Lynchburg in 1887 by the Virginia Baptist State
Convention.   Along with Hartshorn Memorial Institute (1884-
1923), they have rendered outstanding educational assistance
to Black Virginians for many years.   The three institutions
provided much of the leadership that was instrumental in establishing and maintaining support of the Black Baptist secondary schools in Virginia from 1887 through academic year
1956-57.

There is no doubt as to the valuable educational service rendered the Black people of Virginia by the thirteen Black Baptist secondary schools. By 1910, fifty years after the date when most Blacks of Virginia were found to be illiterate, more than 70 percent of the total 671,096 Black population were able to read and/or write. The rise in literacy from nearly naught to 70 percent was a remarkable accomplishment, even for fifty years. It was one for which much credit is due both the Black people, who were eager to learn, and the Christian Church, which was inspired to help them do so.

Had it not been for the church, the education of the Black race in Virginia would have been practically nonexistent for many years after the Civil War. Had it not been for the Black Baptist church, during the same period, the education of the Black race at the secondary level, and concomitantly the acculturation process, would have been seriously hindered.

As a result of the Supreme Court decision of 1954, which ruled that schools throughout the nation were to be desegregated, most of the Black Baptist secondary schools closed at the end of academic year 1954-55. One school, the Bluestone Harmony Academic and Industrial School at Keysville, Virginia, remained open until 1957, when it was forced to close due to low enrollment. The closing of the school at Keysville brought to a close the end of an era that spanned nearly three-fourths of a century, an era in which the Black Baptists of Virginia contributed immeasurably to the cultural advancement of Black Virginians.

REFERENCES

Chapter I

[1]Clarence Holte, Education of Blacks in America: A Brief History (Norfolk, Virginia: Journal and Guide Publishing Company, 1974), p. 4.

[2]John H. Russell, The Free Negro in Virginia, 1619-1865 (Baltimore: Johns Hopkins Press, 1913; reprint, New York: Dover, 1969), p. 40. The classes of free Black children that received special educational advantages during the Colonial period were: 1) children born of free Black parents; 2) mulatto children born of free Black mothers; 3) mulatto children born of white servant or free women; 4) children of free Black and Indian mixed parents; and 5) manumitted slaves. The most prominent class of mulattoes was of slave women parentage, but such children were slaves. Both classes of free mulattoes indicated at (2) and (3) above were the product of illegitimacy, since laws of the Virginia colony prohibited interracial marriages, slave or free.

[3]Ibid., pp. 64-65.

[4]Ellwood P. Cubberly, The History of Education (New York: Houghton Mifflin, 1920), pp. 679-680.

[5]Russell, pp. 64-65.

[6]Michael B. Katz, Class, Bureaucracy, and Schools: The Illusion of Educational Change in America (New York: Praeger, 1971), pp. 1-55. Katz is a historian whose works The Irony of School Reform (1968) and School Reform: Past and Present (1971) were widely acclaimed by scholars as significant contributions to history and educational theory.

[7]Ibid.

[8]Ibid.

[9]Holte, p. 4.

[10]Eric Lincoln, Chronicles of Black Protest (New York: American Library, 1969), p. 37.

[11]William W. Hening, Statutes at Large of Virginia,

13 vols. (New York: R. and W. G. Barton, 1823), 1: 532;
2: 48, 165, 166, 180, 198, and 204.
    12E. Franklin Frazier, The Negro Church in America
(New York: Schocken, 1972), p. 6.
    13Carter G. Woodson, The Education of the Negro
Prior to 1861 (Washington, D. C.: Associated Publishers,
1919; reprint, New York: Arno and the New York Times,
1968), p. 29. Carter G. Woodson (1875-1950) was a Virginian
and the son of an ex-slave. He was educated at Berea College, University of Chicago, and Harvard University, where
he received the Ph. D. degree. Woodson was a pioneer Black
historian who founded the Association for the Study of Negro
Life and History (Washington, D. C.) in 1915. In 1916, he
founded the Journal of Negro History. Three years later, in
1919, he founded the Associated Publishers. Notable among
his contributions to American history are: A Century of Negro
Migration, History of the Negro Church, The Negro in Our
History, The Rural Negro, Negro Makers of History, African
Heroes and Heroines, and Negro Orators and Their Orations.
    14Ibid. , p. 30.
    15Ibid.
    16Ibid. , p. 3.
    17Carter G. Woodson, The Negro in Our History (Wash-
ington, D. C.: Associated Publishers, 1941), p. 103.
    18Ibid. , p. 105.
    19Ibid.
    20Ibid.
    21Charles W. Dabney, Universal Education in the South,
2 vols. Chapel Hill, North Carolina: University of North
Carolina Press, 1936; reprint, New York: Arno and the New
York Times, 1960, 1: 25-26. Dr. Dabney, with J. L. M.
Curry, Dr. E. A. Alderman, Dr. Charles McIver, Dr. H. B.
Frissell, George Foster Peabody and Rev. Wallace Buttrick
served as a charter member of the Executive Board of the
Southern Education Conference. The conference, founded on
June 1, 1901, at Winston-Salem, had as its purpose the promotion of the "industrial and general education of the colored
people. "
    22William W. Hening, Statutes at Large of Virginia,
3 vols. (New York: R. and W. G. Barton, 1823), 3: 87.
    23Ibid. , p. 453.
    24Dabney, p. 40.
    25Benjamin Quarles, The Negro in the American Revo-
lution (Chapel Hill, North Carolina: University of North Carolina Press, 1961), p. 95.
    26Ibid.
    27Ibid. , p. 85.

[28]Dabney, 1: 10-19.
[29]Woodson, The Negro in Our History, p. 103.
[30]Frazier, pp. 8-9.
[31]Carter G. Woodson, The History of the Negro Church
(Washington, D. C. : Associated Publishers, 1972), p. 27.
[32]N. H. Pius, An Outline of Baptist History (Nashville,
Tennessee: National Baptist Publishing Board, 1911), pp. 51-
55.
[33]Norman R. Yetman, Life Under the "Peculiar Institution" (New York: Holt, Rinehart and Winston, 1970), pp.
181-184. This book is a compendium of slave narratives collected under auspices of the Federal Writers' Project, of the
Works Progress Administration, Washington, D. C. , in 1941.
Henry Johnson, an ex-slave from Virginia, was interviewed at
St. Louis in 1937, when he was slightly over ninety years of
age. He recalled that when he was enslaved at Patrick County,
Virginia, his master made all of the hundred and twenty-five
slaves he owned get in the road on Sunday and walk five miles,
one way, to church. Buggies, with members of the master's
family, were scattered throughout the column of marchers to
keep them from running away. When they arrived at the
church, they were required to sit on logs on the outside in
the boiling sun, while a white man preached to them the same
message repeatedly: "Niggers, obey your masters and mistresses, and don't steal from 'em. "
[34]Pius, p. 57.
[35]R. B. Semple, History of the Rise and Progress of
the Black Baptists in Virginia (Richmond, Virginia: Publisher
Unknown, 1810), p. 30. Book was researched at the Virginia
State Archive, Richmond.
[36]Woodson, The History of the Negro Church, p. 46.
[37]Ibid. , p. 47.
[38]Herbert Aptheker, A Documentary History of the
Negro People in the United States (New York: Citadel, 1971),
p. 28.
[39]Benjamin Brawley, Negro Builders and Heroes (Chapel
Hill, North Carolina: University of North Carolina Press,
1965), p. 42.
[40]Joanne Grant, Black Protest (Greenwich, Connecticut:
Fawcett, 1968), pp. 38-41.
[41]Woodson, The Education of the Negro Prior to 1861,
pp. 112-133; and Dabney, Universal Education in the South, 1:
26.
[42]Ibid. ; and John Hope Franklin, From Slavery to
Freedom: A History of Negro Americans, 3d ed. , enl. , (New
York: Vintage, 1969), p. 210.
[43]Joseph A. Tate, A Digest of the Laws of Virginia

(Richmond, Virginia: Publisher Unknown, 1841), p. 124.
Book was researched at the Virginia State Archive, Richmond.
[44]Franklin, pp. 212-213.
[45]Woodson, The Negro in Our History, pp. 282-283.
[46]Ibid. , p. 288.
[47]Brawley, p. 200.
[48]Aptheker, pp. 70-71.
[49]Ibid. The full text of the resolution is contained in Appendix B.
[50]Woodson, The Education of the Negro Prior to 1861, p. 170.
[51]Luther P. Jackson, Free Negro Labor and Property Holding in Virginia, 1830-1860 (New York: Atheneum, 1962), p. 20.
[52]Frederick Law Olmsted, The Slave States (New York: Capricorn, 1959), p. 88.
[53]Woodson, The Education of the Negro Prior to 1861, p. 218.
[54]Henry L. Morehouse, Baptist Home Missions in America (New York: George Wheat, Printer, 1883), pp. 388-389.
[55]Woodson, The History of the Negro Church, p. 160. One of the most noteworthy and effective means of struggle against the institution of slavery was the renowned "Underground Railroad. " The purpose of the organization was to help slaves flee from southern slavery into the North, usually to Canada. It operated in flagrant violation of the Fugitive Slave Law. The first traces of this movement began to take shape around 1800. By 1860, the movement had reached large proportions with many thousands of slaves having traveled it to freedom.
[56]Ibid. , p. 8.
[57]Ibid.

Chapter II

[1]Franklin, pp. 270-278.
[2]U. S. Department of Interior, Bureau of Education, Negro Education: A Study of the Private and Higher Schools for Colored People in the United States, by Thomas Jesse Jones, Bulletin 1916, No. 39, vol. 2 (Washington, D. C. : Government Printing Office, 1917; reprint, New York: Negro Universities Press, 1969), p. 658. In response to numerous and insistent demands for information concerning private and higher schools for Blacks, by many persons and agencies to whom appeals had been made for money and sympathy, the

John J. Smallwood, Ph. D.

Elba Baptist Church, in which Pittsylvania Industrial, Normal, and Collegiate Institute was founded.

Two-room Lodge Hall, which housed the Pittsylvania Institute for six months in 1903.

The late Dr. W. L. Ransome and the church he pastored for many years--the First Baptist Church of South Richmond, Virginia.

Graduating class, Ruffin Academy, 1908; Mary Jones, second from right, rear row.

Lincoln Hall, Smallwood-Corey Industrial and Collegiate Institute, Claremont, Virginia. First floor contained administrative offices, dining hall, and kitchen. Second and third floors were residence accommodations for girls.

Campus scene, Bluestone-Harmony Academic and Industrial
School, Keysville, Virginia.

Faculty of the Bluestone-Harmony School, 1926.

Rev. and Mrs. Marcellus Rux, shown in 1927 at Bluestone-Harmony School.

Portion of graduating class, 1932, Bluestone-Harmony School.

Sylvester C. Booker

Rev. W. A. Young

United States Bureau of Education, in cooperation with the
Phelps-Stokes fund made a comprehensive study of the schools,
beginning in 1914.   The task of making the investigation was
placed in the hands of Dr. Thomas Jesse Jones, a graduate
of Washington and Lee University, and Columbia University,
where he received the doctorate of philosophy in sociology.
He spent eight years in the research department of Hampton
Institute and was in charge of the Black statistics for the census of 1910.   The United States Bureau of Education felt that
he, a Welshman by birth, had a certain detached point of view,
which made him the most eligible person to investigate Black
private secondary and higher education in the South.   The in-
vestigating team prepared an exhaustive schedule of questions
in regard to the schools.   Questions were related to their
histories, managerial conditions, religious and social activities, the work of graduates and other students who had been
enrolled, and many others.

3Ibid. , p. 250.

4Franklin, pp. 270-278.

5U. S. Department of Interior, Bureau of Education,
Negro Education: A Study of the Private and Higher Schools
for Colored People in the United States, by Thomas Jesse
Jones, Bulletin 1916, No. 38, vol. 1, (Washington, D. C. :
Government Printing Office, 1917; reprint, New York: Negro
Universities Press, 1969), pp. 5-20.

6Franklin, pp. 270-278.

7U. S. Department of Interior, Bureau of Education,
Negro Education: A Study of the Private and Higher Schools
for Colored People in the United States, by Thomas Jesse
Jones, Bulletin 1916, No. 38, vol. 1, pp. 275-276.

8Morehouse, pp. 398-500.

9Ibid. , pp. 405-407.

10Ibid. , p. 440.

11Woodson, The History of the Negro Church, p. 177.

12Ibid. , p. 129.

13Ibid. , p. 31.

14Joseph T. Wilson, The Black Phalanx (Hartford,
Connecticut: American Publishing Company, 1890), p. 503.
Wilson was the first Black member of the National Council of
Administration of the Grand Army of the Republic.   He served
as a Captain in the 2d Regiment, Louisiana Native Guard
Volunteers, and later in the 54th Massachusetts Volunteers--
the most famous of the Union Black Regiments that engaged
in the Civil War struggle.   In the winter of 1882, when a re-
union of one hundred Black and white men who served in the
Civil War took place at Richmond, Virginia, Wilson was
chosen by his comrades to write the history of the Black

contribution in the great Rebellion. The Black Phalanx is a
monumental treatise. Facts in the book are based on first-
hand knowledge and primary sources.
     [15]Ibid.
     [16]Ibid. , p. 504.
     [17]Ibid.
     [18]Ibid. , pp. 505-507. Lieutenant Trotter's statement
is contained in Appendix C.
     [19]Benjamin Quarles, The Negro in the Making of Amer-
ica (New York: Collier, 1964), p. 128.

Chapter III

     [1]John Richard Dennett, The South as It Is: 1865-1866
(New York: Viking, 1965), pp. v-vi.
     [2]Franklin, pp. 303-305.
     [3]John Hope Franklin, Reconstruction After the Civil
War (Chicago: University of Chicago Press, 1964), p. 29.
     [4]Franklin, From Slavery to Freedom: A History of
Negro Americans, pp. 303-305.
     [5]Edgar A. Toppin, A Biographical History of Blacks
in America Since 1528 (New York: McKay, 1971), pp. 120-
121.
     [6]Ibid.
     [7]Ibid.
     [8]Ibid.
     [9]Ibid.
     [10]Richard N. Current, Reconstruction: 1865-1877
(Englewood Cliffs, New Jersey: Prentice-Hall, 1965), pp. 28-
31.
     [11]Herbert Aptheker, To Be Free (New York: Interna-
tional Publishers, 1969), p. 169.
     [12]Toppin, p. 131.
     [13]Aptheker, To Be Free, p. 169.
     [14]Franklin, From Slavery to Freedom: A History of
Negro Americans, p. 315.
     [15]Emma L. Thornbrough, Black Reconstructionists:
Great Lives Observed (Englewood Cliffs, New Jersey: Prentice-Hall, 1972), p. 13.
     [16]Woodson, The Negro in Our History, p. 413.
     [17]Franklin, Reconstruction After the Civil War, pp. 38-52.
     [18]Ibid.
     [19]Ullin Whitney Leavell, Philanthropy in Negro Educa-
tion (Nashville, Tennessee: Cullom and Chertner, 1930),
pp. 50-52.
     [20]Ibid.
     [21]Pius, pp. 64-65.

[22]Frank P. Lewis, "A History of The Baptist General Association of Virginia (Colored)." (Bachelor of Divinity degree thesis, Virginia Union University, Richmond, 1937), p. 1. (Mimeographed.) Lewis is to be credited with doing original research on this subject through inspecting original documents contained in the libraries of the late Dr. P. F. Morris and Dr. Z. D. Lewis. He also researched the complete minutes of the Virginia Baptist State Convention, extending from 1897 to 1935, which were provided him by the late Dr. George E. Reade of Richmond. Assistance was also provided him by Wallace Van Jackson, former librarian at Virginia Union University, Richmond; Drs. W. T. Johnson and C. C. Scott of Richmond; Dr. A. A. Galvin, Newport News, Virginia; and the late Dr. George Rice Hovey, former President of Virginia Union and resident of Upper Montclair, New Jersey. The complete unpublished thesis was provided this writer by the late Dr. J. Marcus Ellison, who served as an adviser to Dr. Lewis in the preparation of the document.

[23]Ibid., p. 5.

[24]Woodson, The History of the Negro Church, pp. 226-227.

[25]Ibid., p. 244.

[26]Ibid., p. 218.

[27]Frazier, p. 39.

[28]Henry Allen Bullock, A History of Negro Education in the South: From 1619 to the Present (Cambridge, Massachusetts: Harvard University Press, 1970), p. 42.

[29]Ibid., p. 43.

[30]Ibid., pp. 43-44.

[31]Franklin, From Slavery to Freedom: A History of Negro Americans, p. 318.

[32]Ibid., p. 319.

[33]Robert C. Twombly, Blacks in White America Since 1865: Issues and Interpretations (New York: McKay, 1971), p. 30.

[34]Franklin, From Slavery to Freedom: A History of Negro Americans, pp. 317-318; and Horace Mann Bond, The Education of the Negro in the American Social Order (Englewood Cliffs, New Jersey: Prentice-Hall, 1934), p. 56.

[35]U. S. Department of Interior, Bureau of Education, Annual Report of the Commissioner of Education to the Secretary of the Interior, for the Year Ended 30 June 1871, p. 358.

[36]Ibid.

[37]Ibid., pp. 571-572; and U. S. Department of Commerce, Bureau of the Census, Negro Population in the United States, 1790-1915, pp. 375-435.

[38]Ibid.

[39]Ibid.

Chapter IV

[1]U. S. Department of Interior, Bureau of Education, Negro Education: A Study of the Private and Higher Schools for Colored People in the United States, by Thomas Jesse Jones, Bulletin 1916, No. 39, vol. 2, pp. 607-669.

[2]Morehouse, p. 440.

[3]Charles H. Corey, A History of the Richmond Theological Seminary with Reminiscences of Thirty Years Work Among the Colored People of the South (Richmond: J. W. Randolph, 1895), pp. 52-55.

[4]Miles Mark Fisher, Virginia Union University and Some of Her Achievements (Richmond: Virginia Union University, 1924), pp. 32-33. The late Dr. Fisher was the Joseph P. Hoyt Professor of Ecclesiastical History at Virginia Union University when the school celebrated its twenty-fifth anniversary in 1924. He wrote the book in honor of the many dedicated persons who had graduated there. Fisher was a native of Atlanta, Georgia, and a 1918 graduate of Morehouse College Atlanta, where he was valedictorian of his class. A committee, headed by the late C. C. Spaulding, for many years the President of the North Carolina Mutual Life Insurance Company, Durham, called Fisher to the prestigious White Rock Baptist Church, Durham, in 1932. Fisher pastored that church for more than forty years.

[5]Ibid.

[6]Ibid. Dr. Nathaniel Colver died in Chicago on September 25, 1870.

[7]Morehouse, p. 441.

[8]Corey, pp. 52-55; and Morehouse, p. 442. Charter members of the Board of Trustees were Nathan Bishop, A. B. Capwell, J. B. Hoyt, W. A. Cauldwell, H. K. Elyson, Stephen Woodman, J. H. Holmes, Richard Wells, and A. E. Dickinson, the last three of whom were Black. Rev. J. H. Holmes was pastor of the First African Baptist Church, Richmond, having succeeded Dr. Ryland in August 1867. He became the first Black pastor of the church, the membership of which reached four thousand in 1870, under his capable leadership. That same year he was called to serve as a trustee of Richmond Institute. He was a former student of Drs. Colver and Ryland and was highly respected by both. Rev. Wells, also a former student at Richmond Institute under Dr. Colver, was pastor of the Ebenezer Baptist Church, Richmond. He was President of the Virginia Baptist State Convention for several years before becoming a trustee of Richmond Institute. Rev. A. E. Dickinson was pastor of the Leigh Street Baptist Church, Richmond, when he was elected to the Board of

Trustees of Richmond Institute.   It is not known where he ob-
tained his education.
    [9]Morehouse, p. 442.
    [10]Ibid.
    [11]Lewis, pp. 26-27.
    [12]U. S. Department of Interior, Bureau of Education,
Negro Education: A Study of the Private and Higher Schools
for Colored People in the United States, by Thomas Jesse
Jones, Bulletin 1916, No. 39, vol. 2, p. 636.
    [13]Morehouse, p. 442.
    [14]Corey, pp. 152-153.
    [15]Ibid. , p. 139.
    [16]Fisher, p. 35; and Lewis, p. 31.
    [17]U. S. Department of Interior, Bureau of Education,
Negro Education: A Study of the Private and Higher Schools
for Colored People in the United States, by Thomas Jesse
Jones, Bulletin 1916, No. 39, vol. 2, p. 635.
    [18]Fisher, p. 52.
    [19]U. S. Department of Interior, Bureau of Education,
Negro Education: A Study of the Private and Higher Schools
for Colored People in the United States, by Thomas Jesse
Jones, Bulletin 1916, No. 39, vol. 2, p. 635.
    [20]Fisher, p. 52.
    [21]Lewis, pp. 44-50.
    [22]Ibid. , p. 44.   Shortly thereafter, Rev. P. F. Mor-
ris, Chairman of the Educational Board of the Virginia Baptist
State Convention, asked for a financial report of the Education
Finance Committee.   The report is contained in Appendix D.
    [23]Ibid. , p. 45.
    [24]Richmond Planet, April 12, 1890, p. 1.   Newspaper
is on file at the Virginia State Archive, Richmond.
    [25]Lewis, pp. 46-47.
    [26]Ibid.
    [27]Ibid. , pp. 48-49.
    [28]Ibid.   Full text of the Agreement of 1896, the up-
dated "Compact", is contained at Appendix I.   Letter to Rev.
Lewis concerning G. W. Hayes is at Appendix E.
    [29]Ibid. , pp. 49-50.
    [30]Ibid. , pp. 51-54.
    [31]Ibid.
    [32]Ibid. , p. 48.
    [33]Ibid. , pp. 50-56.
    [34]Ibid. , p. 57.
    [35]Ibid. , pp. 57-70.
    [36]Ibid. , p. 72.
    [37]Richmond Planet, May 13, 1899, p. 1.   John H. Mit-
chell, Editor of the Planet, considered the Thirty-Second An-

nual meeting of the Virginia Baptist State Convention to be sufficiently important for him to personally attend the meeting. As a result, he wrote a special article on the conduct of the Convention, which appeared in the May 13, 1899, edition of his newspaper. The complete editorial, as it appeared in the popular Black newspaper, appears in Appendix F. Organization of the Baptist General Association of Virginia (Colored) is described in Appendix G.

[38]Lewis, pp. 70-88.

[39]Ibid. , p. 94.

[40]W. H. R. Powell, Illustrations from a Supervised Life (Philadelphia: Continental Press, 1968), p. 46. The late Dr. Powell was pastor of the well-known Shiloh Baptist Church, Philadelphia, for many years. He knew President Gregory W. Hayes, Virginia Seminary, rather intimately and regarded him as having been a man of great mental stature and excellent leadership ability. During the periods 1926-29 and 1934-36, Powell served as President of Virginia Seminary; on both occasions he continued to occupy the pastorate of Shiloh Baptist Church. He traveled the six hundred miles round trip between Lexington, Virginia, and Philadelphia every weekend that it was possible to do so. Powell had indicated that during the years of his presidency of the seminary, no other person was more outstanding in providing financial assistance, advice, and encouragement than Rev. Richard Bolling of Norfolk. Powell died at Philadelphia in 1976.

[41]Ibid. , p. 112.

[42]Lewis, p. 96.

[43]Ibid. , pp. 100-105.

[44]Ibid.

[45]Ibid.

[46]Ibid.

[47]Interview with the late John M. Ellison, President-Emeritus, Virginia Union University, Richmond, January 10, 1975. Dr. Ellison, a minister who holds a Doctorate of Philosophy from Drew University, was the first Black president of Virginia Union University. When interviewed he was eighty-seven years of age and yet very active in community affairs. A biographical sketch of Ellison is contained in Appendix J.

[48]Lewis, pp. 62-90.

[49]Ibid.

[50]U. S. Department of Commerce, Bureau of the Census, Negro Population in the United States: 1790-1915, pp. 798-840.

[51]W. N. Hartshorn, An Era of Progress and Promise, 1863-1910; The Religious, Moral and Educational Development

of the Negro Since His Emancipation (Boston: Pricilla, 1910), p. 123.

[52]Ibid.

[53]Ibid.

[54]Ibid.

[55]Interview with Evelyn Collins Brown, Richmond, Virginia, January 10, 1975. Brown, a retired public school teacher, is a native of the Eastern Shore of Virginia. She spent half a century teaching at Tidewater Collegiate Institute, Cheriton, and in the public school system at Richmond.

[56]Ibid.

[57]Ibid.

[58]George B. Downing, Newark, New Jersey, personal letter to Lester R. Russell, Farmingdale, New Jersey, April 2, 1975. Personal files of Lester F. Russell. Attorney Downing is now practicing law at Newark, New Jersey.

[59]Interview with Evelyn Collins Brown, Richmond, Virginia, January 10, 1975.

[60]Ibid.

[61]Ibid.

[62]George B. Ruffin, Heathsville, Virginia, personal letter to Lester F. Russell, Farmingdale, New Jersey, February 5, 1975. Personal files of Lester F. Russell. Ruffin is the youngest of eleven children born to the late Rev. J. R. Ruffin and his wife, Martha Ellen. George Ruffin was graduated from Ruffin Academy in 1908 and began teaching in 1909. While teaching, he attended Virginia State College, Petersburg, and received the Bachelor of Science degree. He is an outstanding educator, who recently retired after teaching more than fifty-two years in King and Queen and Caroline counties, Virginia. In 1969, he was appointed Assistant Superintendent of Schools for Caroline County, a position he held until he retired in 1971. Currently, he is serving a second term as an elected member of the Northumberland County (Virginia) School Board.

[63]Ibid.

[64]Ibid.

[65]Ibid.

[66]Mary B. Jones, Indian Neck, Virginia, personal letter to Lester F. Russell, Farmingdale, New Jersey, January 21, 1975. Personal files of Lester F. Russell. Jones is a graduate of Ruffin Academy, in the class of 1909. She received a degree in Elementary Education from Virginia State College, Petersburg, in 1948. She taught at Ruffin Academy for one year and in the public schools of King and Queen County, Virginia, for more than fifty years. She is now

retired and compiling a history of the local Baptist Association. Jones was acquainted with Rev. J. R. Ruffin for many years. She admired and respected him as a man of high moral character and superior intellect.
[67]Watson R. Harvey, Sr., "My Life; Who Am I?," a booklet prepared for distribution to the membership of the church he pastored for many years, First Mount Olive Baptist Church, St. Stephens Church, Virginia, March 15, 1974, p. 3. Rev. Harvey is now deceased; however, when interviewed in 1975, he was ninety-six years of age and very alert and active in church and community affairs. He was also a great poet, who prepared a poem for the youth of Mount Olive when he was ninety-six. For nearly three-fourth of a century, this gentle, God-fearing man went through life farming, preaching, and teaching school in King and Queen County, Virginia. Many young men and women throughout the nation owe him a debt of gratitude for his unselfish devotion to their welfare.
[68]Ruffin, personal letter.
[69]Jones, personal letter.
[70]Harvey, personal letter.
[71]Ruffin, personal letter.
[72]Ibid.
[73]Ibid.
[74]Ibid. To include the children and grandchildren of this couple, there were more than twenty-five descendants of the Ruffin family who attended either Ruffin Academy or King and Queen Industrial High School. Nineteen of that number became teachers and other professionals. A son, the late H. M. Ruffin, D.D., was chosen Rural Minister of the Year, in 1957, by Emory College, Atlanta, Georgia. In the same year, he was honored by the Virginia Polytechnic Institute, Blacksburg, Virginia, for excellence as a teacher, social worker, minister, and lecturer. Dr. Ruffin was a graduate of Virginia Union University.
[75]U.S. Department of Commerce, Bureau of the Census, Negro Population in the United States: 1790-1915, pp. 585-700.
[76]Sylvester C. Booker, "History of the Northern Neck Industrial Academy," prepared at Northern Neck Academy, Ivondale, Virginia, 1934, pp. 4-5. (Typewritten.) Booker was Principal of the Academy from 1929 through 1934. Information cited is based on an unpublished history compiled by Booker during his administration as Principal. The material was presented to the author during a personal interview with Booker at his home in Richmond January 8, 1975. Booker is now retired, having served more than forty-five years as a teacher and administrator in Virginia schools.

[77]Ibid., pp. 6-7.

[78]Ibid., pp. 5-6.

[79]Ibid.

[80]Ibid.

[81]Ibid.; and U. S. Department of Interior, Bureau of Education, Annual Report of the Commissioner of Education to the Secretary of the Interior, for the Year Ended 30 June 1906, pp. 1151-1173.

[82]Booker, pp. 9-14. Booker indicated that it was common for organizers of Black schools to include "industrial" in school titles as philanthropic agencies were more amenable to giving financial assistance to those schools that were industrially oriented.

[83]Interview with Booker.

[84]Ibid.

[85]Ibid.

[86]Ibid.

[87]Interview with Ellison.

[88]U. S. Department of Interior, Bureau of Education, Negro Education: A Study of the Private and Higher Schools for Colored People in the United States, by Thomas Jesse Jones, Bulletin 1916, No. 39, vol. 2, p. 658.

[89]Booker.

[90]Interview with Booker.

[91]Interview with Ellison.

[92]U. S. Department of Commerce, Bureau of the Census, Negro Population in the United States: 1790-1915, pp. 792 and 835.

[93]U. S. Department of Interior, Annual Report of the Commissioner of Education to the Secretary of the Interior, For the Year Ended 30 June 1905, p. 1159.

[94]U. S. Department of Interior, Bureau of Education, Negro Education: A Study of the Private and Higher Schools for Colored People in the United States, by Thomas Jesse Jones, Bulletin 1916, No. 39, vol. 2, p. 658.

[95]Mattie C. Rux, Detroit, Michigan, personal letter to Lester F. Russell, Farmingdale, New Jersey, September 30, 1975. Personal files of Lester F. Russell; Samuel M. Thompson, "The Influence of the Baptist Church Upon the Education of the Negro in Virginia" (Master of Science thesis, Virginia State College, Petersburg, 1945), p. 22; and A. B. Caldwell, History of the American Negro: Virginia Edition, vol. 5, (Atlanta: A. B. Caldwell, 1921), pp. 254-257. Mrs. Mattie Rux is the widow of the late Rev. Marcellus Rux.

[96]Rux, personal letter.

122   Black Baptist Schools in Virginia

97U. S. Department of Commerce, Bureau of the Census, Negro Population in the United States: 1790-1915, pp. 793-837.

98Lewis, pp. 100-107.

99Ibid.

100U. S. Department of Interior, Bureau of Education, Negro Education: A Study of the Private and Higher Schools for Colored People in the United States, by Thomas Jesse Jones, Bulletin 1916, No. 39, vol. 2, p. 659.

101U. S. Department of Commerce, Bureau of the Census, Negro Population in the United States: 1790-1915, pp. 793-837; and interview with General Johnson, Richmond, January 11, 1975.

102Interview with General Johnson, Richmond, January 11, 1975; and W. R. Harvey, Newtown, Virginia, personal letter to Lester F. Russell, Farmingdale, New Jersey. Personal files of Lester F. Russell. Johnson is a former Principal of the Rappahannock Industrial Academy, 1934-42.

103Interview with Johnson.

104Ibid.

105U. S. Department of Interior, Bureau of Education, Negro Education: A Study of the Private and Higher Schools for Colored People in the United States, by Thomas Jesse Jones, Bulletin 1916, No. 39, vol. 2, pp. 631-632; and interview with Johnson. Johnson reiterated that the word "industrial" was carried in secondary school titles to gain financial assistance from philanthropists who favored the Booker T. Washington philosophy of industrial training for Blacks, as indicated by Sylvester Booker. Many school founders of the era included "industrial" in the school name, but few offered industrial courses, according to Johnson. This was particularly the case when school officials found that individuals or agencies that made grants to private schools did not require industrial training as a requisite to receiving funds. Johnson asserted that many Blacks did not support Booker T. Washington's belief that they should receive industrial training instead of learning Greek, Latin, French, etc.

106Interview with Johnson.

107Ibid.

108Ibid.

109Ibid. The three Doctors Robinson are brothers. Their father was the second principal of Rappahannock Industrial Academy, Ozeana, Virginia.

110Thompson, pp. 35-40.

111Caldwell, pp. 54-56.

112Ibid.; and U. S. Department of Interior, Bureau of Education, Negro Education: A Study of the Private and Higher

Schools for Colored People in the United States, by Thomas Jesse Jones, Bulletin 1916, No. 39, vol. 2, pp. 651-652.
[113]Charles E. Jones, Gretna, Virginia, personal letter to Lester F. Russell, Farmingdale, February 15, 1975. Personal files of Lester F. Russell; and Clyde H. Banks, Gretna, Virginia, personal letter to Lester F. Russell. Charles Jones is President of the Pittsylvania Historical Society, Chatham, Virginia.
[114]Ibid.
[115]Thompson, p. 43.
[116]Ibid.
[117]A. P. Young, "Caroline Baptist Sunday School Union, 1922: Revised History 1952," prepared at Shiloh Baptist Church, Bowling Green, Virginia. (Handwritten.) The late Rev. Young was a member of the Caroline Baptist Sunday School Union for more than sixty years. He was more than ninety years of age and pastoring Shiloh Baptist Church when an interview was conducted on January 12, 1975. He is a graduate of the Bowling Green Industrial Academy, class of 1906. He is also a graduate of Virginia Seminary, Lynchburg, class of 1911.
[118]Interview with Young.
[119]Young. See Appendix A for copy of original document prepared in 1922 with portions updated in 1952, by the late Rev. Young.
[120]Ibid.
[121]Ibid.
[122]Ibid.
[123]Ibid.
[124]Ibid.
[125]Ibid.
[126]Ibid.
[127]Ibid.
[128]Ibid.
[129]Ibid.
[130]Ibid.
[131]Ruffin, personal letter.
[132]Young.
[133]U. S. Department of Commerce, Bureau of the Census, Negro Population in the United States: 1790-1915, pp. 403-836.
[134]Jones, personal letter.
[135]Ibid.
[136]Ibid.
[137]Fisher, p. 105.
[138]Paul E. Bowes, "Historical Background of Secondary Education in Fredericksburg, Virginia," prepared at Fredericksburg, 1940. (Typewritten.)

[139]J. C. Grant, Sr. , Thirty-Second Annual Bulletin of Mayfield High School Located at Fredericksburg, Virginia, 1936-1937 (Fredericksburg: Charles Carmichael Printing Company, 1937), p. 2.

[140]Bowes.

[141]Ibid.

[142]Ibid.

[143]Grant, Sr. , p. 2. Biographical sketch of Dr. W. L. Ransome is contained in Appendix J.

[144]Caldwell, pp. 35-38.

[145]Interview with W. L. Ransome, Richmond, Virginia, January 10, 1975. The late Dr. Ransome was ninety-six years of age at the time the interview was conducted, yet extremely alert and articulate. Within one month, in early February 1975, Dr. Ransome died.

[146]Grant, Sr. , p. 3.

[147]Bowes.

[148]Ibid.

[149]Ibid. George Vick was Princiapl when the author was graduated from Mayfield High School in the class of 1936.

[150]Ibid. Roster of 1936-37 student body is contained in Appendix K.

[151]Grant, Sr. , pp. 9-10.

[152]Ibid. , p. 7.

[153]Bowes.

[154]Interview with Ransome.

[155]Biographical sketches of Walker, Grant, and Bowes are contained in Appendix J.

[156]U. S. Department of Commerce, Bureau of the Census, Negro Population in the United States, 1790-1915, pp. 375-840.

[157]Bernyce O. Wynn, Suffolk, Virginia, personal letter to Lester F. Russell, Farmingdale, New Jersey, February 12, 1975. Personal files of Lester F. Russell. Wynn, a member of the First Baptist Church, Suffolk, has compiled information on the Nansemond Collegiate Institute in the interest of preserving its history. Some of the individuals who provided her with information were at one time connected with the Institute. Records on the history of the school were not available in writing.

[158]Ibid.

[159]Ibid. ; and U. S. Department of Interior, Bureau of Education, Negro Education: A Study of the Private and Higher Schools in the United States, by Thomas Jesse Jones, Bulletin 1916, No. 39, vol. 2, p. 660.

[160]Wynn, personal letter.

[161]Ibid.

162Ibid.
163Ibid.
164Ibid.
165Caldwell, pp. 266-268.
166Ibid.
167Ibid.
168Euan G. Davis, Claremont, Virginia, personal letter to Lester F. Russell, Farmingdale, New Jersey, November 20, 1975. Personal files of Lester F. Russell. Davis now owns the site on which the Institute was located.
169Caldwell, p. 243.
170Davis, personal letter; and Welton J. Henderson, Norfolk, Virginia, personal letter to Lester F. Russell, Farmingdale, New Jersey, October 29, 1975. Personal files of Lester F. Russell. Henderson is the son of the late Rev. H. M. Henderson.

Chapter V

1W. E. B. Dubois, The Common School and the Negro American (Atlanta: Atlanta University Press, 1911), p. 15.
2Ibid.
3U. S. Department of Commerce, Bureau of the Census, Negro Population in the United States: 1790-1915, pp. 403-429. The Bureau of Census has explained that the 90 percent statistic was an estimate. The Bureau of Education, United States Department of Interior, has stated in Bulletin 1916, No. 38, vol. 1, subject, "A Study of Private and Higher Schools for Colored People in the United States," 1917, that census statistics compiled before 1870 were highly inaccurate. The basis for the classification of persons as literate or illiterate was the ability of those ten years of age and older to write in some language, regardless of the ability to read. When specific answers were not obtained to inquiries directed to Blacks, census takers assumed they were unable to write and classified them as illiterate. This was not the case with inquiries directed to whites that were not returned. The assumption was made that whites were literate, and they were so classified even when they did not respond to inquiries. It is likely that far more Blacks were literate in 1860 than were reported to be. Population statistics for 1860 (United States) are contained in Appendix L. A map showing where the schools were located is contained in Appendix M.
4Ibid. , pp. 835-840; and Dubois, pp. 128-130.
5Katz, pp. 1-55.

APPENDIX A

History of the Caroline Sunday School Union,
by A. P. Young (1952)

The Negro Baptist Churches have an organizational set up peculiar to themselves. Among such bodies are found Women's
Conventions, Church School and B. T. U. Conventions, and Sunday School Unions. These organizations are forces that make
for racial improvement, as they employ both the willing and
the trained people of our groups as leaders and teachers, and
develop character and solidarity by furnishing modes of expression for their deepest thoughts and feelings.

To use one of these organizational forces in the development of the religious life of his people and to promote
cooperative Bible in Caroline County, the Rev. J. H. Turner,
B. D. , a graduate of the Richmond Theological Institute, and
pastor of the Shiloh Baptist Church, Bowling Green, Va. ,
after consultation with Deacon Wilson C. Young and some other
leading Sunday School superintendents, organized the Caroline
Baptist Sunday School Union in 1893, with the following named
Sunday Schools as charter members: Shiloh, Bowling Green;
Jerusalem, Sparta; St. Paul, Delos; and St. John, Milford.

The officers of this new body were Rev. J. H. Turner,
president; Deacon James Baylor, first vice president; Deacon George Lonesome, second vice president; Brother C.
H. Smith, recording secretary; and Brother Lewis Monte,
treasurer. As time moved on, Sister Lucy Graves, a
teacher in the public school system of Caroline County,
succeeded Brother C. H. Smith as Recording secretary,
and Brother H. P. Latney became the treasurer.

In the year of 1895 the Rev. J. H. Turner resigned his

127

church and left the county. Thereupon, the work of the Caroline Sunday School Union began to lag. To remedy this situation some of the leading members of the Union sought and urged the Rev. R. W. Young, the dynamic pastor of the First Mount Zion and the Ebenezer Baptist Churches, to accept the presidency of the Union and to revive the work thereof. The Rev. Mr. Young told the Brethren in his usual straightforward manner that if the Union would undertake the task of building and operating an academy to furnish secondary education for the colored youth of his county, he would accept the office.

This new idea struck a responsive chord in the breasts of such leading churchmen as Deacon George Lonesome, Deacon James Baylor, Deacon R. B. Fortune, Deacon Montgomery Wright, Deacon W. L. Young, and Brother London Myers. These brethren led in electing Rev. R. W. Young second president of the Caroline Sunday School Union and with him incorporated the dynamic idea of building a school into the agenda of the Union.

With this new program the Caroline Sunday School Union began its unique career, and employed its powers so assiduously to the promotion of private and public education that Sunday School work fell into the second place.

The Union surrounded its new president, Rev. R. W. Young, with the following officers: Brother London Myers, first vice president; Deacon George Lonesome, second vice president; Miss Maggie Upshaw, a graduate of the Virginia Normal and Industrial Institute, recording secretary; and Deacon R. B. Fortune, treasurer.

President Young and his cabinet found that the Union had a depleted treasury of only $3.56 and a membership of three Sunday Schools. But they set themselves to work with so much zest that during the following six years the membership was increased to eleven or twelve Sunday Schools and a definite effort was made to purchase a site for the proposed academy. The first tract of land purchased contained 19 3/4 acres, and was bought from Mr. Deighler at a cost of $500.

As the Union did not have some of the money needed for the purchase of the land, Rev. R. W. Young and Deacon R. B. Fortune borrowed the amount required from Mr. O. P. Smoot and made themselves personally responsible for the payment of the loan until the Union could raise the money and pay for it.

To this end the Union staged a rally, in which it offered a banner to the Sunday School raising and reporting the
largest amount of money.   Shiloh   Secondary School, Bowling
Green, was awarded the banner in this financial effort that
netted the Union $215.92.

The loan from Mr. Smoot was paid and the Union immediately commenced to assemble material for the erection of
the first school building.   Again Rev. R. W. Young and Deacon R. B. Fortune secured money for the Union's building
program by negotiating a loan from Mr. Mark Beasley, securing the deal with their personal notes.

The first building was a frame structure which served
as a girls' dormitory, class rooms, and chapel.   It has been
named Young's Hall, and was well enough completed by the
fall of 1903 to be used for school purposes.   The Rev. R. W.
Young, like Barnabas of old who went to Tarsus to seek Paul
to take charge of the missionary work at Antioch, went to Essex County, found the Professor L. L. Davis, who was at
that time principal of the Champlain Industrial High School,
and brought him to Caroline County to become the first principal of the Bowling Green Industrial Academy.   This school
opened its doors to receive students October 4, 1903 and enrolled 41 students during the session of the school.   In the
spring of 1904, the Bowling Green Industrial Academy was
chartered by the State Corporation Commission, with E. C.
Moncure being the patron of the act.   From this time onward
the property of the Union was managed for it by the Bowling
Green Academy Corporation.   Trustees were appointed according to the charter which read in part as follows: "The names
of the trustees who shall manage the affairs of this corporation for the first year and until their successors are chosen
shall be R. W. Young, R. B. Fortune, W. C. Young, T. M.
Allen, E. A. Johnson, James Baylor, George Lonesome, L.
L. Davis, D. C. Winston, J. M. Beverly, W. L. Davis, and
W. J. Young. "   The first four of these gentlemen were di-
rectors.

The Union operated the school under the name of the
Bowling Green Industrial Academy for eleven years.   During
this time the cost of instruction, repairs and upkeep of the
buildings, and boarding and lodging of the students was borne
by this body.

A well which was the gift of Dr. T. M. Allen was dug
and it served the school well for many years.   During these

eleven years the trustees purchased in all 30 acres of land, 7 3/4 acres of which were bought from a Mr. Luther Scott by Principal L. L. Davis with money given to the school by one Miss Frances E. Wright.

As worthy as this physical achievement is, it is surpassed many times by the personal worth and work of the twenty-one graduates, and other undergraduates who studied at the Union's school. The names of those who passed from the halls of the Academy wearing the badge of graduates are as follows: J. Ryland Byrd, 1904; Conway O. Myers, 1905; Nettie Baylor, Victoria Baylor, Martha Paige, Mary E. Young, and Andrew P. Young, 1906; Bessie M. Myers and John J. Washington, 1908; Robert J. Banks, Rev. Eldous L. R. Guss, Edward Turner, Stephen R. Young, Maggie Johnson, Viola Young and Elkanah Young, 1909; Carrie E. Young, Mabel N. Coleman and Edith Gray, 1910; Arthur J. Thomas, 1911; and Cora P. Berry, 1912.

These persons are truly sons and daughters of the Union and merit a place of mention in her history. For some time there had been arising in Virginia a tidal wave of public sentiment in favor of the state providing high school instruction for her citizens. This fact coupled with the dire need of schools to train teachers for the schools of the state, led Division Superintendent, John Washington, to seek aid for the struggling Academy, from the Slater Fund. But as this assistance could be obtained only for schools under public control, he advised the Union through Principal L. L. Davis to turn the Bowling Green Academy over to the County School Board. In compliance with this request the Union turned over 10 acres of land and the buildings thereon to the Caroline County School Board to be used for the Secondary training of the Youth of the county in the year 1914.

However, the Union continued to cooperate with the School Board in running the school that was renamed the Caroline Training School. She furnished the major part of the fuel needed, and operated the boarding and lodging departments exclusively.

Prof. G. Hayes Buchanan became the principal of the Caroline Training School and Prof. L. L. Davis accepted the position as teacher of Agriculture.

During the years that the Union operated the Academy, deficits in operating expenses had been occurring. And now,

that the management of the school had passed into the hands
of the county, the Union found herself faced with the necessity
of readjusting her affairs.   This called for a change in the
administration and Deacon W. L. Young was elected president
of the Union; Stephen R. Young, who had served as recording
secretary, was succeeded by the Rev. L. L. Davis and Deacon R. B. Fortune, who had nobly and efficiently manned the
post of treasurer, gave place to Brother C. R. Lewis.   Having fully adjusted the financial obligations, Deacon W. L.
Young resigned and Brother London Myers was elected President in his stead.   During the new administration the third
large school building was erected and paid for with money
raised by the Union; a gift of $1600 from the Rosenwald Fund;
and the proceeds of $5000 left to the Bowling Green Academy
by the late Miss Frances E. Wright.   Brother Meyers super-
intended the construction of this building in person.   The educational work at this time was directed by Professor A. M.
Walker for 9 years and Rev. H. M. Ruffin for 2 years.   In
1926, Brother H. P. Latney became the president of the
Union.   It was during his administration that Deacon R. B.
Fortune, a friend of the cause of education, and a man who
held the clearest concept of the importance of an accredited
four year high school of any of his contemporaries, organized
the Caroline County wide league to raise funds for a new
building to be used as an auditorium and dormitory.   President Latney personally collected more than $200 by using the
spade that was used in breaking the ground for the new building as the core of a spade fund; and secured a gift of $100
from the County Supervisors for the new auditorium.

In 1926 Rev. Hovey R. Young A. B. , B. D. , became the
principal of the Caroline Training School.   He soon began to
concentrate upon qualifying the school for accreditation.   This
goal was reached in the first two years of his administration.
In 1928 the name of the school was changed for the third time
to mark the upward trend in its growth.   Principal Young appointed a committee of some of his faculty members to select
a name for the newly accredited high school.   Mrs. Gertrude
N. Young, a graduate of Hampton Institute and the faithful wife
of Rev. A. P. Young, suggested that the school should be
called Union High School in commemoration of what the Caroline Sunday School Union had done to bring it into being.   The
name was so appropriate that it was unanimously accepted by
the Committee of the Faculty, and just as readily adopted by
the Caroline County School Board.   In the fall of 1926 the
Rev. A. P. Young was elected to the trustee board of the
Caroline Baptist Sunday School Union.   His unassuming, sacri-

ficial service elevated him to the chairmanship of this board
in 1931. From that time onward his intrepid leadership
brought about permanent recognition in an advisory capacity
for the trustee Board of this Union with the Caroline County
School Board in matters concerning the welfare of Union High
School, and placed him in a position to secure lasting benefits
for the public school system in general, such as, buses for
the transportation of school children and annual contracts for
the County School Board's responsibility to furnish fuel for
the heating of all school houses. It was also under his leadership that the Union wrote its closing chapter in cooperating
with the School Board in the operation of Union High by trans-
ferring all the land held by the Union to the Caroline County
School Board, and the granting of a deed of correction to the
said Board and others who had purchased land from the Union
during the period of adjustment. In 1936 Brother O. W. Latney, who had served for 2 years as recording secretary, was
elected president of the Union; Brother Thomas Hardman became recording Secretary and served for 2 years. Then the
secretaryship passed into the hands of the present incumbent
Brother Percey C. Saunders. The administration of Brother
O. W. Latney may be aptly termed a period of reconstruction:
for by the relinquishment by the Union of her hold upon the
material, she has seized more firmly an agenda that makes
for the spiritual advancement of our people. Bible study is
being fostered, educational institutions are being helped, and
missionary work is being done. Her interest in public education led to the creation of a scholarship fund.

The Caroline Sunday School Union has inspired and
brought forth a group of Christian workers who have immor-
talized their names by what they have done for education and
missions. Among these mention is made of Brother Jas. B.
Young, the founder of the old Ideal Club which inspired boys
and girls of the teen age to sacrifice for the cause of education. This club raised more than $600 to equip the office of
the Bowling Green Industrial Academy. Mrs. Rosa Thomas
Byrd, Mrs. Lizzie B. Washington, Mrs. Allie R. Latney,
Mrs. Daisy B. Young, and Mrs. Elizabeth Vaugham, under
the caption of volunteer missionaries, raised more than $500
to furnish the room in the auditorium and dormitory at Union
High School which has been dedicated to their memory. During the years that the Union was actively engaged in educational work it raised and collected from other bodies and
sources the following sums of money:

The Union raised	$14,379
The Mattaponi Association	11,000
Caroline County wide League	10,500
The Rosenwald Fund	1,600
Miss Frances Wright's estate	4,886

Total $42,359

The greater part of this money was invested in land, buildings and equipment. Therefore, when awareness of the duty of the state to furnish public high school education to the boys and girls of her citizenry caused the Union to shift her burden to the shoulders of the county, she transferred to its ownership property valued at $35,000.

-- A. P. Young

APPENDIX B

Free Blacks Oppose Colonization Scheme, 1817

A group of Blacks who opposed the Colonization scheme, met at Richmond, Virginia, on January 24, 1817, and made the following statement:

At a meeting of a respectable portion of the free people of color of the city of Richmond, on Friday January 24, 1817, William Bowler was appointed Chairman, and Lentley Craw, Secretary. The following preamble and resolution were read, unaminously adopted, and ordered to be printed:

Whereas a Society had been formed at the seat of government for the purpose of colonizing, with their own consent, the free people of color of the United States; therefore, we the free people of color of the City of Richmond, have thought it advisable to assemble together under the sanction of authority, for the purpose of making a public expression of our sentiments on a question in which we are so deeply interested. We perfectly agree with the Society, that it is not only proper, but would ultimately tend to the benefit and advantage of a great portion of our suffering creatures, to be colonized; but we thus express our approbation of a measure laudable in its purposes, and beneficial in its designs, it may not be improper in us to say, that we prefer being colonized in the most remote corner of the land of our nativity, to being exiled to a foreign country--and whereas the president and board of managers of the said society have been pleased to leave it to the entire discretion of Congress to provide a suitable place for carrying these laudable intentions into effect--Be it therefore Resolved, that we respectfully submit to the wisdom of

Congress whether it would not be an act of charity to grant
us a small portion of their territory, either on the Missouri
River, or any place that may seem to them most conducive
to the good and our future welfare, subject however, to such
rules and regulations as the Government of the United States
may think proper to adopt.

APPENDIX C

"The Schoolmaster in the Army"

by Lieutenant James Trotter

Of the many interesting experiences that attended our colored
soldiery during the late war none are more worthy of being
recounted than those relating to the rather improvised schools,
in which were taught the rudimentary branches. One would
naturally think that the tented field so often suddenly changed
to the bloody field of battle, was the last place in the world
where would be called into requisition the schoolteacher's services; in fact it would hardly be supposed that such a thing
was possible. Yet in our colored American Army this became
not only possible but really practicable, for in it frequently,
in an off-hand manner, schools were established and maintained, not only for teaching the soldiers to read and write
but also to sing, nor were debating societies, even, things
unheard of in the camp life of these men. Besides in quite
a number of the colored regiments military bands were formed,
and under the instruction of sometimes a band teacher from
the north, and at others under one of their own proficient fellow soldiers, these bands learned to discourse most interesting music in camp, and often by their inspiring strains did
much to relieve the fatigue occasioned by long and tiresome
marches. But we are speaking now mainly of the work of the
school teacher proper. And what shall we say of the halls of
learning in which were gathered his eager pupils? Well, certainly these would not compare favorably with those of civil
life, as may well be imagined. As says Bryant, truly and
beautifully speaking of primitive religious worship:

"The groves were God's first temples. "

So, too, in the groves and fields of their new land of liberty,

136

these men found their first temples of learning, and in spite
of all inconveniences these school tents were rendered quite
serviceable. Of the text books used there is not much to say,
for these were generally 'few and far between.' Books were
used at times, of course, but quite as often the instruction
given was oral. That these spare facilities did not render
the teacher's efforts ineffective was abundantly proven in the
service, and has been proven since in civil life. Scattered
here and there over this broad country today are many veteran
soldiers who are good readers and writers, some of them fair
scholars, who took their first lessons from some manly fellow
soldier in the manner mentioned, during such camp intervals
as were allowed by the dread arbitrament of war. In a number of regiments these fortunate intervals were quite frequent
and of long duration, and in such cases, therefore, much progress was made.

It must, of course, be remembered that in our colored
regiments a very large percentage of the men were illiterate
especially in those composed of men from the South and so
lately escaped from under the iron heel of slavery. Indeed,
in many of them there could scarcely be found at the com-
mencement of the service a man who could either read or
write. Many an officer can recall his rather novel experience
in teaching his sergeant enough of figures and script letters
to enable the latter to make up and sign the Company morning
report. All honor to those faithful, patient officers, and all
honor, too, given to those ambitious sergeants who after awhile
conquered great difficulties and became educationally proficient
in their lines of duty.

In this connection I readily call to mind one of the most,
if not the most unique figure of all my experience in the army.
It was Colonel James Beecher, of the famous Beecher family,
and a brother of Henry Ward Beecher ... Colonel Beecher,
when encamped neglected no opportunity to form schools of instruction for his men, in order that they might become not
only intelligent, efficient soldiers, but also intelligent, self-
respecting citizens should they survive the perils of war.

I know another ex-colonel and scholar, of high rank as
a man of letters and in social life, who yielding to the call of
duty, not less to country than to struggling race, left his con-
genial studies and took command of a colored regiment, becoming not only their leader, but as chance afforded, their
school-teacher also ... I refer to that true and tried friend
of the colored race, Colonel T. W. Higginson.

But let it not be supposed for a moment that only officers and men of another race were engaged in this noble work of school teaching in our colored army. Not a few of the best workers were colored chaplains, who wisely divided their time between preaching, administering to the sick by reason of wounds or otherwise, and to teaching the old 'young idea how to shoot'; while many non-commissioned officers and private soldiers cheerfully rendered effective service in the same direction. Nor must we close without expressing warm admiration for those earnest, ambitious soldier pupils who, when finding themselves grown to man's estate, having been debarred by the terrible system of slavery from securing an education, yielded not to what would have been considered only a natural discouragement, but, instead, followed the advice and instruction of their comrade teachers, and bending themselves to most assiduous study, gained in some cases great proficiency, and in all much that fitted them for usefulness and the proper enjoyment of their well-earned liberty. And so we say, all honor to teachers and taught in the Grand Army that made a free republic, whose safe foundation and perpetuity lies in the general education of its citizens.

Report of Treasurer, Committee

Educational Board

Virginia Baptist State Convention

July 28th, 1888

Rev. T. J. Chick

Dear Bro
I Has bin trying the Recpts
corect of the Education Finance
Committee at you city I find
by the Minuts th thay Kept as
Having Recvd $391. 91

I Recivd at Lynchburg -	$324. 91
Since of A Bing from New Yourk	35. 00
again --	4. 00
Making	$363. 91

Bro Barksdale Say He Has

in His Hands for you	7. 00

and Says you Have

in your Hands	14. 00
Making	$384. 91

Paid to orders	$265. 83		
in Hand	98. 08		
in your Hands as			
abov exped	21. 00	-	119. 08
in all	$384. 91		

Now Plese grat a corect
order from the Educationl Board
for -- one Hundrad and ninteen
and Eight cents and I will
Send it to you-----acknolejing
the ($21. 00)   Yours in Christ

J. E. Farrar   Trs
B. S. Convention

No 808 N 4 St.

APPENDIX E

Letter to Rev. Z. D. Lewis from M. MacVicar, American Baptist Home Mission Society, concerning the alleged recalcitrance of Professor Gregory W. Hayes, President of Virginia Seminary, Lynchburg. Hayes campaigned vigorously for race independence and threatened to organize the Baptists of Virginia for racial independence against those who sympathized with white support for Black education.

Dr. Z. D. Lewis had written to Dr. MacVicar to seek Hayes's reappointment as President. His letter prompted this reply, which was a forerunner to the big Baptist split that was to occur at Lexington, Virginia, on May 10, 1899.

September 27th, 1898
New York, New York

Rev. Z. D. Lewis, D. D.
202 E. Leigh Str.
Richmond, Va.

My dear Brother:

I have received and read with special care your letter of September 24th in which you state that Professor Hayes is very anxious to remain as President of Virginia Seminary at Lynchburg, and is willing to make any concessions, give any pledges or offer any apologies that may be required in order to reinstate him in the confidence of the officers of the Home Mission Society; and you ask me to let you know what concession is desired of him. I need not say to you that I have

140

given a great deal of anxious thought to this matter and have
had numerous consultations with Dr. Morgan; and we are both
of us now, and have been exceedingly desirous simply to do
that which is best for the educational interests of the Negroes
of Virginia. Neither of us has any personal animosity towards
professor Hayes, and we do not wish him any harm whatever.
Indeed, both of us used our influences to have him appointed
to another educational position outside of Virginia.

As you know very well, the Home Mission Society in
addition to the large sums that it has already expended in
Virginia and the great expense of the Institutions which it is
maintaining for the benefit of your people is now about to begin the erection at Richmond of one of the finest groups of
College Buildings to be found anywhere in the South, which
will cost not less than $100,000. Work is to be commenced
on them within the next few weeks. We believe that the Union
University at Richmond can be made one of the best schools
of the kind in the world, provided, simply, that the plans
which have already been so carefully matured, and so enthu-
siastically approved by the Negroes of Virginia, are fully
carried out. These plans contemplate a union of effort; a
union that shall not be on the surface, but that shall be thorough and heartfelt. It is an effort at Co-operation in the
broadest, most liberal and best meaning of that term. The
plan contemplates making of the school at Lynchburg a better
school than it has ever been made, but a school entirely sub-
ordinated to the University at Richmond; a school where the
best possible kind of preparatory work shall be done. From
the beginning of this enterprise the officers of the Home Mission Society have done everything that they knew how to do to
make the plan a success, and they have striven in every possible way to secure the cordial, efficient co-operation of Professor Hayes. We have had his repeated protestations that he
was in sympathy with the plan and his promises to cooperate
heartily, but we have felt from the beginning that his co-operation was not honest; and that his influence has been on the
whole thrown against the Plan of Co-operation. Lynchburg has
been a sort of hot bed of racism. The whole tendency of Professor Hayes' remarks to the students, and his private influence both in Lynchburg and elsewhere, has been to foster a
spirit in opposition to co-operation; a spirit which, as we
think, is harmful to you and your people--as we very clearly
see,--and as he apparently does not, will not and can not see.

We have been very slow to take any action in the matter, or to reach any decision opposed to Prof. Hayes, and

his supporters and friends.   We did not want to be put in the
attitude of opposing him personally, and we were also slow to
take the position of opposing out and out the spirit for which
he stands,--that of foolish independence and self assertion and
of appealing to the weakest elements of his people.

But we have slowly, deliberately and finally reached
this decision; that we will not consent to recommend to the
Executive Board the appointment of Professor Hayes to any
position in connection with the educational work in Virginia.
And so long as he remains connected with the Virginia Seminary I feel certain that our Board will withhold any and all
appropriations for that Institution.

This is a matter of very great importance, and one
that cannot be passed over lightly.   We are now laying founda-
tions for the educational system of Virginia that will last for
a thousand years, and we are maturing plans that cannot well
be changed after they are in operation.   We think, and we
think it very emphatically, that if Virginia Seminary is to be
rescued from its present perilous condition and put upon a
solid foundation, and made capable of doing the work that it
ought to do for the Negroes of the State, it will be necessary
that the Faculty shall be re-organized, the course of study
reconstructed and the Board of Trustees so changed that those
on it shall be in such sympathy with the spirit of cooperation
that they will not need to be asked to give pledges for their
future conduct, but that they will heartily and aggressively cooperate to the fullest extent in the tremendous task that we
have before us in the State.

You perhaps do not know what we know, that it is a
matter of exceeding great difficulty for the Home Mission Society to bear the tremendous burden that it is now carrying
for Negro Baptists of Virginia, and unless we can have not
only the sympathy but the moral and financial support of every
friend of the Cause in the State, there is danger that the work
will suffer loss.   You cannot afford, my dear brother, to take
any attitude which will excuse the conduct of those who stand
in the way of the success of this movement.

I am very sorry for President Hayes; that is, I am
sorry for his short sightedness.   Dr. Morgan and I both have
talked with him personally and laid out before him as plainly
as could lay it before a brother, that there was but one road
to success in this matter; but he has not seen fit to follow
our advice, and constituted as he is, he cannot follow it.   He

is a race man through and through.   He is unable to look at
things from any other point of view than the one that he has
so assiduously cultivated.   No pledges that he may give, no
promises that he may make, no apologies that he can offer,
will change the fact that he believes through and through that
the Negroes can and ought to stand alone, and do their own
work independently of the white people; and so long as he believes this he cannot be an honest man and pretend to believe
something else and offer to work in harmony with those who
believe directly the opposite.   Perhaps he is not to blame for
this, as the saying is, "he is built that way"; but there stands
the fact, which you know just as well as we know.   Now there
are just two courses left for him, so far as we can see.   If
he can have the support of the Board of Trustees he can enter
upon an independent fight in behalf of Lynchburg, which will
divide the forces of the State, perpetuate and increase the an-
tagonisms that we have been trying to heal, and, --fail in the
end.   Or, he can take another course, which we believe he
will take if he is a sincere friend of the Cause that he pro-
fesses to love; viz., he will recognize the inevitable, quietly
and peacefully retire from the position that he now holds, and
thus make it possible for a conference between the officers of
the Home Mission Society and the representatives of the State
Convention looking to a radical readjustment of the whole matter.

Yours very sincerely,

(signed) M. MacVicar
Supt. Education
American Baptist Home Mission
Society

P.S.   You are at liberty to make any use of this letter that
you see fit; and I have sent a copy of it to other parties interested in the same line that you have indicated in your
letter.

(signed) M. MacVicar

[This letter is credited to Dr. Frank P. Lewis, who obtained
it from the files of Dr. Z. D. Lewis.]

APPENDIX F

The Richmond Planet
Vol. XVI No. 23, Richmond, Virginia
Saturday, May 13, 1899

The Baptists at Lexington

THE VIRGINIA SEMINARY AS AN ISSUE, ---
PRESIDENT HAYES WINS OUT.
THE NATIONAL BAPTIST CONVENTION
ENDORSES.
THE PUBLISHING HOUSE SECURES MATER-
IAL HELP - A WARM SESSION, MUCH DEBATE -
A LANDSLIDE SENTIMENT.

Lexington, Va. May 10, 1899

The first Baptist Church of Lexington, Va., is one of
the finest structures in the state. It was handsomely decorated
with wreaths and flowers. President (H. H.) Mitchell called
the meeting to order promptly at 9 o'clock.

After the religious exercises, a short prayer service
was proceeded with. The address of welcome was delivered
by Rev. W. T. Johnson, B. D., on the part of the church and
Rev. Lewis Howe (White) on the part of the mayor and citizens.

He spoke at length

The latter spoke at length upon the beauties and advantages of Lexington. He pitied the civil government which was
not governed and actuated by the Bible.

He declared that there was no color line in sin and no
color line in righteousness.

144

He thought that the problems would be settled by Christian love.   He declared that both races should unite to condemn lawlessness in whites and the blacks should condemn lawlessness in black and both condemning lawlessness in both, we would be carrying out the principles contained in the blessed Bible.

Dr. Williams Responded

Rev. Henry Williams, D. D. of Petersburg, Va. , responded on behalf of the convention.   He gave some valuable statistical information.

He said that there was much talk about race feeling but the convention had come here to know nothing but the love of God and Him crucified.

We accept the welcome of the town, not as Negroes or Afro-Americans but as American citizens.

We come here as a part of the sixty or seventy millions of the American nation.

The President's Address

President H. H. Mitchell delivered his annual address. He said that he had much to say, but had decided that ye (convention) cannot bear them now.

He deplored the decadence of the spirit of Christianity in the convention and the failure of its sessions to be followed by revivals.   President Mitchell said that he would make no recommendations.   He had many things to say, but would not say them now.

During the afternoon session the question which had arisen during the morning session on the enrollment of delegates arose and Rev. Dr. Wesley F. Graham of Richmond led the controversy.   The president ruled that only three members from each church would be entered upon the roll.   He appointed Mr. David Gilbert Jacox of Norfolk to assist Rev. Dr. J. W. Kirby, the corresponding secretary.

The Fight on the Roll of Delegates

Rev. B. F. Fox, D. D. of Salem, offered a substitute that four others, whose names he presented, should be also named to assist.

The president ruled this out and this was no sooner done than Dr. Graham was ready with a motion that Rev. Barnard Tyrell and Rev. W. T. Hall be added to the committee.

Dr. P. F. Morris, Dr. R. Spiller, and Dr. Z. D. Lewis opposed, but it was finally passed.

This was a signal victory for the opposition led by Rev. Dr. Graham. Then continued one of the most stormy debates ever seen in the convention. During these debates occurred some of the stormiest scenes ever known during the history of the convention.

The Issue Defined

Rev. Z. D. Lewis, D. D. , Rev. P. F. Morris, D. D. , Rev. R. Spiller, Rev. H. L. Barco, Rev. Dr. J. M. Armistead, represented the element known as the "Anti-Virginia Seminary, " while Rev. Dr. Graham, Rev. B. F. Fox, D. D. , Rev. Harvey Johnson, D. D. , Rev. Henry Williams, D. D. , John Mitchell, Jr. were on the other side.

The former were in favor of retaining that institution (Va. Seminary) under the management of the American Baptist Home Mission Society (White) and electing a Board of Trustees who would be in favor of electing a successor to Professor G. W. Hayes in keeping with this policy.

The other side was in favor of electing trustees who would sustain Prof. Hayes.

The Troubles at Lynchburg

Another feature in the controversy and which had much to do with the movement was the disagreements in Lynchburg, where differences existed between the Court St. Baptist Church and the 8th St. Baptist Church.

The former sent a large delegation with Rev. R. T.
Hoffman its pastor at its head, while the latter was represented by the ex-pastor of Court St. Baptist Church, Rev.
Dr. Morris and Deacon John Pride. The attempt on the part
of the opposition to re-elect successors to Rev. Dr. Fox and
Rev. Dr. Chisolm on the Board of Trustees of Virginia Seminary, also added to the complications and tended to increase
the majority against the present administration.

Dr. Bowling's Fine Report

The annual sermon was delivered by Rev. R. H. Bowling, D. D. (Norfolk, Va.), Subject "A GREAT GOD AND GREAT
THINGS. " He showed the power and greatness of God by dis-
cussing astronomy, and giving the computed distances of the
planets. He practically paralyzed all hearers by his deliver-
ance of an illustrated sermon, inasmuch as he had brought
forward a framework on which was tacked drawings of his own
creation explaining his discourse as he proceeded. It was the
ablest sermon ever delivered before that body.

After the sermon, business was proceeded with, the
committee on nomination making its report.

No sooner had it done so than Dr. Graham was on his
feet, with a motion to substitute another. It was carried.
Dr. B. F. Fox read the list of names nearly all of the old
officers withdrew and President Mitchell put the motion that
the recording secretary be instructed to cast the vote of the
convention therefor. It was carried.

The newly elected officers are: President, Rev. R. H.
Bowling, D. D. , Norfolk; 1st Vice President, Rev. W. F.
Graham, D. D. , Richmond; 2nd, Rev. B. W. Tyrell, Lynch-
burg; 3rd, Rev. L. B. Ball, Lancaster; 4th, Rev. R. C. Fox,
Harrisonburg; Recording Secretary, Rev. G. O. Coleman,
Manchester; Corresponding Secretary, Rev. A. S. Thomas,
Richmond; Treasurer, R. T. Hill, Richmond.

The convention was adjourned after electing trustees
for Virginia Seminary.

The Virginia Seminary was discussed (at the convention) and the opening speech was made by Rev. Dr. Graham.
On his motion (the seminary) was eliminated from the compact

with the American Baptist Home Mission Society and the Board of Trustees was empowered to secure a new charter.

It is the intention (of the new executive officers) to broaden the scope of the work (of the seminary) and to give the New England states, Pennsylvania, Maryland, District of Columbia and West Virginia representation on the Board of Trustees.

The newly elected trustees are all in favor of President G. W. Hayes.

The amount of money raised was $1645, notwithstanding that several of the dissatisfied brethren carried their money back home.

At the closing of the convention the most friendly feeling prevailed. The outlook is that there will be complete harmony in the ranks of the colored Baptists of the United States.

APPENDIX G

Organization of the Baptist General

Association of Virginia (Colored)

The Baptist General Association of Virginia was organized in the First Baptist Church of Richmond in June 1899, when the "cooperationists" met to discuss the results of the "Lexington meeting. " Rev. James H. Holmes was then pastor of that church. R. Wells was elected Moderator, and they began immediately to evolve plans for the policy of the Association. A distinct advantage was to be had in the fact that there was a oneness of purpose in that meeting. Every man there was a staunch cooperationist. The General Association was organized specifically to carry out the "Compact" with the Society, which had been rejected by the State Convention at Lexington. The purpose of the Association included also cooperation with the Southern Baptist Convention, the Baptist General Association of Virginia (white), and the American Baptist Publication Society. In 1905, when the constitution was adopted, the cooperation clause was made much broader, viz. ,

> Co-operating with such other Baptist organizations for Christian benevolence as shall fully respect the independence and equal rights of the churches [Addenda, Article II, p. 154, Minutes Baptist General Convention].

The first Annual Session was called to order, October 18, 1899, in Lynchburg at the Eighth Street Baptist Church, of which Dr. P. F. Morris was pastor. The gathering was not as large as in the previous meeting with the First African Baptist Church. There were represented thirty-two churches, one society, one Association (Union Baptist), and fifty delegates, of which seventeen were from Danville and Pittsylvania

County. The officers elected were as follows: Moderator, Rev. R. Wells, Ebenezer Baptist Church, Richmond; Vice Moderators, Rev. E. Watts, B. D., Harrison Street Baptist Church, Petersburg; Rev. Isaac Lee, Eastern Shore; Rev. Daniel Cave, Rev. J. W. Booth, Gloucester; Rev. R. B. Hardy, B. D., Mt. Zion Baptist Church, Charlottesville; Rev. M. A. Pannell, Chatham; Corresponding Secretary, Rev. R. C. Quarles, First Baptist Church, Charlottesville; Statistical Secretary, Rev. H. W. Childs, B. Th., Portsmouth; Recording Secretary, Rev. W. M. Moss, B. D., Royal Street Baptist Church, Danville; Treasurer, Dr. A. Binga, Jr., First Baptist Church, Manchester.

APPENDIX H

Commentary on the Black Baptist
Church, by Dr. Frank Lewis

The last decade of the nineteenth century was not only a period of schism and strife in the Negro Baptist Church, but it
was also the period in which the organizing tendency among
Afro-Americans reached its height in Virginia.   Social and
religious institutions sprang up all over the state.   Banks,
insurance companies, benevolent societies, and various other
business concerns were organized.   Many of them were merely
social abortions, which were smothered before they were born.
In nearly every case, Baptist ministers were either the organizers or chief executives of these concerns.   For instance,
Z. D. Lewis was the first President of the Southern Aid Society, which was organized in 1893 in the Second Baptist
Church, of which he was pastor; W. F. Graham, pastor of
the Fifth Street Baptist Church, was president of the Richmond Beneficial Insurance Company, which was organized in
1895; and Evans Payne, pastor of the Fourth Baptist Church,
was a chief executive of the Nickel Savings Bank in Richmond.
Thus, when the General Association was formed, it presented
no peculiar historical significance.

APPENDIX I

The Agreement of 1896 (Norfolk, Virginia)

(This Agreement represents a refinement of the "Compact" entered into at Charlottesville, Virginia, 1891, by the Virginia Baptist State Convention and the American Baptist Home Mission Society.)

The following resolutions were adopted by the Virginia Baptist State Convention when it met in its twenty-ninth session at Norfolk, Virginia in 1896:

Whereas, By special act of the Virginia Legislature, there has been incorporated the Virginia Union University at Richmond, having for its prime object the unification and increased efficiency of the educational work among the Afro-American Baptists of Virginia; and,

Whereas, The Richmond Theological Seminary, the Divinity School of said University, and Hartshorn Memorial College, the Women's College of said University are in successful operation; and,

Whereas, it is proposed to organize at as early a day as practicable a college for men corresponding to that for women; and,

Whereas, it is proposed to bring the Virginia Seminary at Lynchburg and the Spiller Academy, now located at Hampton, into affiliation with the University, and,

Whereas, the trustees of said University, at such time as money can be obtained for that special purpose, propose to organize such additional departments of Law, Medicine, etc., as may be required; and,

Whereas, the American Baptist Home Mission Society, which for more than thirty years had done so much in Virginia for the education of Afro-Americans, offers to cooperate in founding, sustaining, and developing said University; and,

Whereas, The founding and maintaining of such an institution of learning as this will involve the outlay of a very large amount of money and will require, doubtless, many years for its development; and,

Whereas, The success of this enterprise requires the endorsement, active co-operation and the continued financial support and patronage of the Afro-American Baptists of Virginia, for whose special and sole benefit this work is undertaken; therefore,

Resolved, That the Virginia Baptist State Convention, assembled at Norfolk, May 22, 1896, does hereby express its hearty and unqualified approval of the plans for said Virginia Union University, and pledges its active, earnest, and continued cooperation in carrying these plans into successful operation.

Resolved, Second; That this Convention recommends to the Afro-American Baptists of Virginia that they contribute, in cash and interest-bearing notes, payable in installments, the principal to mature not later than January 1, 1900, a sum of not less than $35,000; the first $15,000 of which shall be used for the erection and furnishing of a suitable dormitory for the proposed Men's College, and the remainder of the sum, viz., $20,000, be given toward the liquidation of the indebtedness of Virginia Seminary and the completion and furnishing of its present building, provided that if more than $35,000 be raised and subscribed, the excess thereof shall be divided equally between the Men's College of said University, Virginia Seminary and Spiller Academy; this $35,000 to be regarded only as an earnest of what will eventually be done by the Afro-American Baptists of Virginia for this great central school of Christian learning established for the benefit of them and their children.

Resolved, Third; That this Convention urgently recommends also to the Afro-American Baptists of Virginia to contribute annually, in a liberal manner, for the support of teachers in the proposed Men's College, Virginia Seminary and Spiller Academy, and that the sum thus contributed will be divided into five equal parts, two parts of which shall be given to the Men's College, two parts to Virginia Seminary, and one part to Spiller Academy.

Resolved, Fourth; That the Educational Board of the Convention be, and it is hereby instructed and directed to take such active steps as it may deem wise and necessary to raise the said $35,000; that it put forth earnest efforts to promote the organization of Educational Societies in all the Baptist Churches of Virginia; and that, for the purpose of effectively doing its work, it select and nominate a financial agent to the Trustees of said University, who shall be appointed by said Trustees, and who shall be charged with the responsibility of carrying into effect the plans of the Educational Board for raising the said $35,000 and such other sums as will be required for the support of teachers in each of the said three schools.

The Spiller Academy, of which Dr. G. E. Read was then principal, ratified the "Compact" by adopting the following resolutions drafted by P. F. Morris:

Whereas, By Section Three of the Charter of Virginia Union University provision is made to receive into affiliation with the University Colleges, professional schools, seminaries, or academies; and,

Whereas, the Virginia Baptist State Convention has given its hearty and unqualified approval to the plans of the said Virginia Union University, and has pledged its active and earnest and continued cooperation in carrying these plans into successful operation; and,

Whereas, The said Convention has given its approval and pledged its support to said University with the understanding that Virginia Seminary and Spiller Academy are to be affiliated with said University, and participate in all the benefits accruing from such affiliation; and,

Whereas, The said Convention has also coupled Virginia Seminary and Spiller Academy with the Men's College of said University in its recommendations to the Afro-American Baptists of Virginia to contribute liberally of their means for the support of those schools; now, therefore, be it

Resolved, That the Board of Trustees of Spiller Academy does hereby respectfully apply to the constituted authorities of said Virginia Union University for affiliation thereto and, for participation in all the rights, privileges and immunities which accrue from such affiliation in accordance with Section Three of the Charter of said University, and such regulations as the Trustees of the University may require.

Resolved, That the secretary of this Board is hereby directed to transmit immediately this preamble and resolution to the secretary of the Board of Trustees of said University with the request that action may be taken thereon at as early a day as possible.

APPENDIX J

Biographical Sketches

John M. Ellison

John M. Ellison was born in Northumberland County, Virginia, February 2, 1889. He completed his high school training at Virginia Normal and Industrial Institute (now Virginia State University) in Ettrick. He received the Bachelor of Arts degree from Virginia Union University, Richmond, in 1917; Master of Arts degree from Oberlin College, Oberlin, Ohio, 1927; and Ph. D. from Drew University, Madison, New Jersey, 1933. He was pastor of the Shiloh Baptist Church, Northumberland County, from 1912 to 1926.

From 1917 to 1918, he was Principal of the Northern Neck Industrial Academy, and from 1918 through 1926 Moderator of the Northern Neck Baptist Association. He was professor of sociology and director of religious activities at Virginia State University from 1927 to 1934. He was pastor of the First Baptist Church, South Orange, New Jersey, from 1931 to 1934, and pastor of Zion Baptist Church, Washington, D. C., from 1934 to 1937.

From 1928 through 1934, Dr. Ellison did special research work in rural sociology at Virginia Polytechnic Institute in Blacksburg. In 1936, he was appointed professor of philosophy and social science at Virginia Union University. In 1941, he became the first Black President of Virginia Union University. One of his first outstanding achievements as President was the erection of the Belgian Friendship Building at a cost of approximately one quarter of a million dollars.

Dr. Ellison is the author of The Negro Church in Rural

Virginia, 1930; Negro Organization and Leadership in Rural
Virginia, 1933; Rural Negro Life in Virginia, 1864-1934; The
Hamitic Bible, 1940; and The Art of Friendship, 1943.

Dr. Ellison died at Richmond on October 14, 1979.
The world has lost a dedicated citizen; the Baptist world has
lost a staunch leader.

William Lee Ransome

Dr. W. L. Ransome was born in Nottaway County (Crewe),
Virginia, March 7, 1879, the son of the late Rev. George
and Lucy Ransome. At an early age, he was brought to Richmond, where he attended public school and gained considerable
recognition as a scholar. To obtain a higher education he attended Richmond Theological Institute and became a minister.

In the early days of his career, around 1902, he became pastor of the Shiloh New Site Baptist Church in Fredericksburg. His ministry was very productive and is still remembered. While serving as pastor there, he became recognized for his educational competence when he became a teacher
in Mayfield High School. During that dual service as teacher
and pastor, he continued his education at Virginia Union University toward further degrees. He resigned the pastorate at
Fredericksburg to become pastor of the First Baptist Church
in South Richmond.

For twenty-six years, Dr. Ransome was an instructor
at Virginia Union University. He taught Bible, logic, and
other courses in philosophy. As a classroom teacher, he was
widely known as a scholarly person with an unusual skill as a
teacher. He had a law degree, and took advanced courses in
the philosophy of education and a large variety of theological
disciplines.

Dr. Ransome's long years of ministerial and teaching
service were filled with many accomplishments. He had influential national affiliations. As an author, he had many articles and books to his credit. He was the editor of the Bee
Hive, The Masonic Journal. He founded the Baptist Herald
and was its editor for many years.

W. L. Ransome died at his home in February 1975.

Jason C. Grant, Sr.

Jason Clifton Grant, Sr., was a distinguished citizen of Fredericksburg, Virginia, who was loved and highly respected by his fellow townspeople.

Fredericksburg was his adopted home. He was born in Chatham, Ontario, Canada, on January 9, 1861. His parents were Jason Clifton Grant, a runaway slave from Kentucky, and Sarah Elizabeth (Stevens) Grant, a freeborn woman who came to Canada with her family from Montclair, New Jersey. There were eight children in the Grant family. After the death of his mother, Grant and his brother John, then small boys, were taken to Pontiac, Michigan. Here they lived with relatives and attended public school. After a few years in Pontiac, young Jason was brought back to Chatham by his father. Here he continued his public school education and for three years attended Wilberforce Educational Institute. On the death of his father, he was removed from school and sent to live and work for Dr. A. R. Abbott, an outstanding surgeon, who exerted a highly beneficial influence upon the boy.

As a young man, Grant earned his living primarily as a waiter. In the summer of 1882, he met in a hotel in Saratoga Springs, New York, Joseph Russell, a teacher from Falmouth, Virginia, close to Fredericksburg. So impressed was Russell with Grant's learning and character that he persuaded Grant to come to Fredericksburg and seek a position as teacher. They arrived on August 20 of that year. No doubt because of Russell's influence, Grant almost immediately found a suitable position.

Grant made the community in which he found himself his home. In 1884, he became a naturalized citizen of the United States. On March 28, 1889, he married Evelyn Lucretia Hailstalk, the daughter of John Hailstalk and Lucretia (Evans) Hailstalk, both freeborn, and shortly thereafter bought a home. From this union, there were three children: Charles Stevens Grant, who died early in childhood; the late Jason Clifton Grant, Jr., Associate Professor of English, Emeritus, at Howard University; and the late Carolyn Virginia Grant, Professor of Voice at the same university. Grant had two grandchildren: Jason Clifton Grant III, Reference Librarian at Maryland State College, and Duane Harper Grant, a civil engineer living in Hempstead, New York.

Grant had a long career as a teacher. At first, he

taught in country schools near Fredericksburg and later in those in the city itself. All in all, he taught school for forty-two years. For most of this period he served as Principal of the Fredericksburg Negro schools. He had a great reputation--county- and city-wide--for his extensive and exact knowledge, and for the thoroughness, strictness, and fairness with which he taught.

Grant not only taught school, but engaged in many other activities. During summer months, he worked in hotels in order to supplement his salary as a teacher--thirty dollars per month for ten months (and not always ten). In hotels like those in Saratoga Springs and in White Sulpher Springs, West Virginia, he variously worked as a plain waiter, head private waiter, and secretary to the head waiter.

Moreover, inspired by the contemporary trend toward the development of "Negro business," he was engaged in certain business activities. He helped form a company that operated a brickyard for several years. He was founder and the secretary of the People's Benevolent Association, an insurance company, which operated successfully for many years. He conducted a grocery store. And he invested in real estate on a small scale.

Ranking high--if not highest--among the activities that characterized Grant's life in Fredericksburg were his religious activities. When he was in town and not sick in bed, he attended all of the services of his church--the Shiloh Baptist Church (New Site)--regardless of weather conditions. Similarly he attended many of the services in other Negro churches in town when these services did not conflict with those in his own church. For many years he variously served as trustee, deacon, clerk, and Sunday School superintendent of his church. He was faithful in his participation in the proceedings of such religious conventions as the Lott-Carey Convention and the Sunday School Union, often serving in some office--usually secretary.

He participated in other important activities. He was a first lieutenant in the Fredericksburg Negro unit of the Virginia militia. He was one of the founders and the secretary of the Fredericksburg Normal and Industrial Institute. And he was among those instrumental in persuading city officials to develop this institution into a city high school. He was one of the founders and the secretary of the Shiloh Cemetery Association. He even helped clear and fence the cemetery

grounds. In fact, there was hardly an undertaking of importance among Negroes in and about Fredericksburg during his
day in which he did not participate as a leader.

Shortly after the death of his wife on February 16,
1934, Grant moved to Washington, D. C. , to live with his
daughter Carolyn and to be near his son Jason. Here he
spent his time mainly in attending religious and other meetings
in the city or on the Howard University campus; by visiting
his friends, especially those who were sick in hospitals; and
by enjoying his children and grandchildren. He took special
delight in attending services at Berean Baptist Church, which
he loved and admired, and to which he made important contributions.

Grant died on December 10, 1951, in Washington, D. C. ,
at the residence of his daughter, Carolyn. He was buried in
the Shiloh Cemetery in Fredericksburg on December 12, 1951,
a few short weeks after his ninety-first birthday.

The high esteem in which Grant was held by the Negro
citizens of Fredericksburg is attested to by their gifts and tes-
timonials to him and by the fact that during his lifetime they
named their school for him and Joseph Walker, his close
friend and colleague in many an enterprise.

Joseph Walker

Joseph F. Walker was born at Spotsylvania Court House,
Spotsylvania County, Virginia, on December 17, 1854. He
was the slave of Colonel William Goodwin, a large plantation
owner.

After the Civil War, Walker left the Goodwin plantation
and went to work with a Mr. Haislip, Caroline County, Virginia, for forty dollars and board per year. In 1871, he went
to Fredericksburg, where he obtained work at a paper mill
for $1. 14 per day. In 1873, he purchased ten acres of land
in Spotsylvania County, near Spotsylvania Court House, and
built a cabin on it for his mother.

Walker gave up his paper-factory job in 1873 and moved
to the residence of Judge Barton, Fredericksburg, where he
became his butler. He also became sexton of the church to
which Judge Barton belonged, St. George's Church. The combined income from both jobs amounted to seventeen dollars
per week.

In 1878, Walker was married. A child was born to
the couple in 1879 and lived until 1898. His wife died in
November 1926.

Walker went into mail service in 1909 and relayed mail
to stations in areas surrounding Fredericksburg for more than
twelve years.

Walker spent more than forty-eight years as senior
deacon at the Shiloh New Site Baptist Church, Fredericksburg,
Virginia.

He died at Fredericksburg in 1935.

Frederick D. Bowes

Frederick D. Bowes was also a distinguished citizen of Fredericksburg. He was born in that city on February 22, 1863.
He attended public schools at Washington, D. C. For several
years after completing high school at Washington, he taught
in the public schools of Virginia. After several years, he
went to work with the United States Post Office for greater
security. He retired from the postal service after working
for thirty-one years.

A deacon at the Shiloh New Site Baptist Church, serving alongside Messrs. Walker and Grant, who were also deacons, Frederick Bowes was instrumental in helping to obtain
a new elementary school for the Black citizens of Fredericksburg. He was married and the father of four children. He
died in Washington, D. C. , in 1935.

APPENDIX K

Mayfield High School,
Class Roster of 1936-1937

Abbott, Sylvia	Culpeper, Va.
Anderson, Annie	Fredericksburg, Va.
Butler, Geneva	Haymarket, Va.
Brown, Douglas	Fredericksburg, Va.
Brown, Louise	Fredericksburg, Va.
Brown, Marie	Fredericksburg, Va.
Chapman, Kathleen	Culpeper, Va.
Chambers, Major	Howison, Va.
Childs, Marian Ellen	Fredericksburg, Va.
Coleman, Mary D.	Fredericksburg, Va.
Coleman, Muriel	Howison, Va.
Coleman, Virginia J.	Fredericksburg, Va.
Coakley, Holland	Goby, Va.
Dudley, Bernard	Fredericksburg, Va.
Ellis, Marian	Fredericksburg, Va.
Furguson, James	Fredericksburg, Va.
Ford, Dorothy M.	Fredericksburg, Va.
Gillison, Russel	Fredericksburg, Va.
Gordon, Naomi	Atlantic City, N. J.
Gray, Emmaline	Fredericksburg, Va.
Gray, Vivian	Fredericksburg, Va.
Griffin, Lucile	Fredericksburg, Va.
Hall, Geneva	Caroline County, Va.
Hamn, Arthur	Brooke, Va.
Harris, Bessie	Fredericksburg, Va.
Harrison, Lucille	Stafford, Va.
Hairston, Luvenia	Martinsville, Va.
Henderson, Ada	Fredericksburg, Va.
Howard, James	Fredericksburg, Va.
Jackson, Ella	Culpeper, Va.

162

Jackson, Jeanette	Fredericksburg, Va.
Jackson, John	Fredericksburg, Va.
Jackson, Louise	Fredericksburg, Va.
Johnson, Georgia	Fredericksburg, Va.
Johnson, Walter	Brooke, Va.
Lewis, Margretta	Fredericksburg, Va.
Lewis, Pearl	Fredericksburg, Va.
Lewis, Sarah	Fredericksburg, Va.
Lewis, Walter	Fredericksburg, Va.
Lightfoot, Rhoda	Culpeper, Va.
Lucas, Andrew	Fredericksburg, Va.
Lucas, Clarice	Fredericksburg, Va.
Lucas, Lawrence	Fredericksburg, Va.
Lucas, Robert	Fredericksburg, Va.
Lucas, Virginia	Fredericksburg, Va.
McClendon, Lula	Dumphries, Va.
Noel, Lucy	Fredericksburg, Va.
Parker, Odell	Howison, Va.
Pendleton, Ruth	Fredericksburg, Va.
Pratt, Monroe	Fredericksburg, Va.
Pratt, Theodore	Fredericksburg, Va.
Price, Viola	Culpeper, Va.
Reed, Jacqueline	Fredericksburg, Va.
Roberts, Mary	Culpeper, Va.
Robinson, Clemitine	Fredericksburg, Va.
Roebuck, Rosa	Oak Park, Va.
Rodgers, Margaret	Fredericksburg, Va.
Ross, Annetta	Fredericksburg, Va.
Scott, Alease	Culpeper, Va.
Scott, Bertha	Howison, Va.
Smith, Lillian	Fredericksburg, Va.
Tate, Bessie	Fredericksburg, Va.
Taylor, Augustus	Fredericksburg, Va.
Taylor, Charles	Fredericksburg, Va.
Thornton, Lois	Fredericksburg, Va.
Thompson, Ruth	Culpeper, Va.
Thomasson, Effie	Fredericks Hall, Va.
Washington, Allen	Fredericksburg, Va.
Watts, Lloyd	Fredericksburg, Va.
Watts, Doris M.	Fredericksburg, Va.
Wheeler, Elizabeth	Fredericksburg, Va.
Williams, Addie	Oak Park, Va.
Williams, Douglas	Fredericksburg, Va.
Williams, Mary S.	Fredericksburg, Va.
Willis, Gladys	Summit, Va.
Yates, Naomi	Fredericksburg, Va.

Negro and White Population of the United States in 1860

(Compiled from the Census Returns of 1860)

Negro

State	Slave	Free	White	Total
United States	3,953,760	488,070	26,922,537	31,364,367
Free States	18	225,224	18,512,183	18,737,425
Slave States	3,950,511	250,787	7,936,619	12,127,977
New England		24,711	3,110,480	3,135,191
Maine		1,327	626,947	628,274
New Hampshire		494	325,579	326,073
Vermont		709	314,369	315,078
Massachusetts		9,602	1,221,432	1,231,034
Rhode Island		3,952	170,649	174,601
Connecticut		8,627	451,504	460,131
Middle Atlantic	18	131,272	7,327,548	7,458,838
New York		49,005	3,831,590	3,880,595
New Jersey	18	25,318	646,699	673,035
Pennsylvania		56,949	2,849,259	2,906,208
East North Central		63,699	6,855,644	6,919,343
Ohio		36,673	2,302,808	2,339,481
Indiana		11,428	1,338,710	1,350,138
Illinois		7,628	1,704,291	1,711,919
Michigan		6,799	736,142	742,941
Wisconsin		1,171	733,693	774,864
West North Central	114,931	4,900	1,906,583	2,026,414
Minnesota		259	169,395	169,654
Iowa		1,069	673,799	674,848
Missouri	114,931	3,572	1,063,409	1,181,912
South Atlantic	1,837,260	196,622	3,144,344	5,178,226
Delaware	1,798	19,829	90,589	112,216
Maryland	87,189	83,942	515,918	687,049
Virginia	490,865	58,042	1,047,299	1,586,206
North Carolina	331,059	30,463	629,942	991,464
South Carolina	402,406	9,914	291,300	703,620
Georgia	462,198	3,500	491,550	957,248
Florida	61,745	932	77,746	140,423

Negro

State	Slave	Free	White	Total
East South Central	1,372,913	21,447	2,626,376	4,019,736
Kentucky	225,483	10,684	919,484	1,155,651
Tennessee	275,719	2,690	526,271	964,041
Mississippi	436,631	773	353,899	791,303
West South Central	625,407	19,146	1,102,490	1,727,043
Arkansas	111,115	144	324,143	435,402
Louisiana	331,726	18,647	357,456	708,002
Texas	182,566	355	420,891	603,812
Pacific		4,214	375,337	379,051
Oregon		128	52,160	52,188
California		4,086	323,177	327,263
District of Columbia	3,185	11,131	60,763	75,079
Territories	46	928	310,316	311,290
Nebraska	15	67	28,696	28,778
Kansas	2	625	106,390	107,017
Colorado		46	34,231	34,277
New Mexico		85	82,924	83,009
Utah	29	30	40,125	40,184
Nevada		45	6,812	6,857
Washington		30	11,138	11,168

APPENDIX M

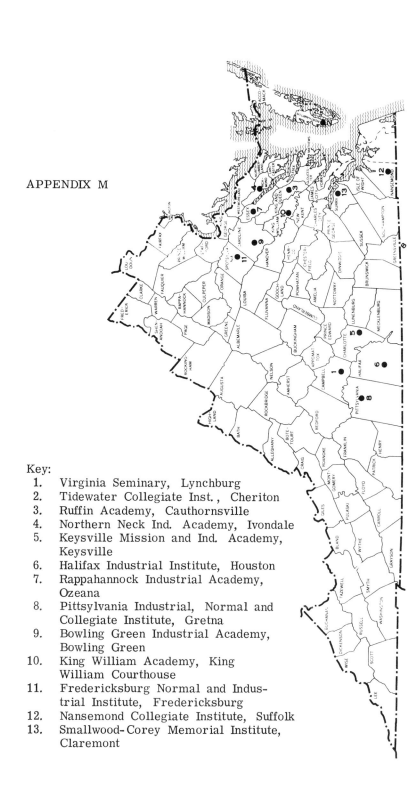

Key:
1. Virginia Seminary, Lynchburg
2. Tidewater Collegiate Inst., Cheriton
3. Ruffin Academy, Cauthornsville
4. Northern Neck Ind. Academy, Ivondale
5. Keysville Mission and Ind. Academy,
   Keysville
6. Halifax Industrial Institute, Houston
7. Rappahannock Industrial Academy,
   Ozeana
8. Pittsylvania Industrial, Normal and
   Collegiate Institute, Gretna
9. Bowling Green Industrial Academy,
   Bowling Green
10. King William Academy, King
    William Courthouse
11. Fredericksburg Normal and Indus-
    trial Institute, Fredericksburg
12. Nansemond Collegiate Institute, Suffolk
13. Smallwood-Corey Memorial Institute,
    Claremont

BIBLIOGRAPHY

I. Primary Sources

A. Official Documents, Records, and Reports

Aptheker, Herbert. A Documentary History of the United States. New York: Citadel, 1971. 2 vols.

Hening, William W. Statutes at Large of Virginia, 1619-1792. New York: R. and W. G. Barton, 1823. 13 vols.

Hofstadter, Richard. Great Issues in American History. New York: Vintage, 1958. 2 vols.

Jones, Thomas Jesse. Negro Education: A Study of the Private and Higher Schools for Colored People in the United States. Bulletin 1916, no. 39. 2 vols. United States Bureau of Education. Washington, D. C.: Government Printing Office, 1917; reprint, New York: Negro Universities Press, 1969. 2 vols.

U. S. Department of Commerce. Bureau of the Census. Negro Population of the United States: 1790-1915. Washington, D. C.: Government Printing Office, 1918.

U. S. Department of Interior. Bureau of Education. Annual Report of the Commissioner of Education to the Secretary of the Department of the Interior for the Year Ended 30 June 1871. Washington, D. C.: Government Printing Office, 1872. 2 vols.

_____. _____. Annual Report of the Commissioner of Education to the Secretary of the Department of the Interior for the Year Ended 30 June 1872. Washington, D. C.: Government Printing Office, 1873. 2 vols.

_____. _____. Annual Report of the Commissioner of Education to the Secretary of the Department of the Interior for the Year Ended 30 June 1873. Washington, D. C. : Government Printing Office, 1874. 2 vols.

_____. _____. Annual Report of the Commissioner of Education to the Secretary of the Department of the Interior for the Year Ended 30 June 1874. Washington, D. C. : Government Printing Office, 1875. 2 vols.

_____. _____. Annual Report of the Commissioner of Education to the Secretary of the Department of the Interior for the Year Ended 30 June 1884. Washington, D. C. : Government Printing Office, 1885. 2 vols.

_____. _____. Annual Report of the Commissioner of Education to the Secretary of the Department of the Interior for the Year Ended 30 June 1887. Washington, D. C. : Government Printing Office, 1888. 2 vols.

_____. _____. Annual Report of the Commissioner of Education to the Secretary of the Department of the Interior for the Year Ended 30 June 1888. Washington, D. C. : Government Printing Office, 1889. 2 vols.

_____. _____. Annual Report of the Commissioner of Education to the Secretary of the Department of the Interior for the Year Ended 30 June 1889. Washington, D. C. : Government Printing Office, 1891. 2 vols.

_____. _____. Annual Report of the Commissioner of Education to the Secretary of the Department of the Interior for the Year Ended 30 June 1893. Washington, D. C. : Government Printing Office, 1894. 2 vols.

_____. _____. Annual Report of the Commissioner of Education to the Secretary of the Department of the Interior for the Year Ended 30 June 1895. Washington, D. C. : Government Printing Office, 1896. 2 vols.

_____. _____. Annual Report of the Commissioner of Education to the Secretary of the Department of the Interior for the Year Ended 30 June 1900. Washington, D. C. : Government Printing Office, 1901. 2 vols.

_____. _____. Annual Report of the Commissioner of Education to the Secretary of the Department of the

Interior for the Year Ended 30 June 1905. Washington, D. C. :
Government Printing Office, 1907. 2 vols.

_____. _____. Annual Report of the Commis-
sioner of Education to the Secretary of the Department of the
Interior for the Year Ended 30 June 1907. Washington, D. C. :
Government Printing Office, 1908. 2 vols.

_____. _____. Annual Report of the Commis-
sioner of Education to the Secretary of the Department of the
Interior for the Year Ended 30 June 1910. Washington, D. C. :
Government Printing Office, 1911. 2 vols.

_____. _____. Annual Report of the Commis-
sioner of Education to the Secretary of the Department of the
Interior for the Year Ended 30 June 1912. Washington, D. C. :
Government Printing Office, 1913. 2 vols.

_____. _____. Annual Report of the Commis-
sioner of Education to the Secretary of the Department of the
Interior for the Year Ended 30 June 1916. Washington, D. C. :
Government Printing Office, 1916. 2 vols.

B. Newspapers and Periodicals

    Afro-American (Baltimore), 1905-1955.

    The Baptist Home Mission Monthly, 1888-1899.

    Freedman's Record.

    Journal and Guide (Norfolk), 1905-1955.

    Richmond Planet, 1890-1900.

C. Articles, Memoirs, Travel Accounts, Reports, and
    Miscellaneous Writings

        Andrews, Sidney. The South Since the War. Boston:
Ticknor and Fields, 1866; reprint, Boston: Houghton Mifflin,
1970.
        Aptheker, Herbert (ed.). The Education of Black Peo-
ple by W. E. B. Dubois, 1906-1960. New York: Monthly
Review, 1973.
        Billington, Ray A. (ed.). The Journal of Charlotte
Forten. New York: Collier, 1967.
        Bond, Horace Mann. The Education of the Negro in
the American Social Order. Englewood Cliffs, New Jersey:
Prentice-Hall, 1934.

Booker, Sylvester C. "History of the Northern Neck Industrial Academy. " Ivondale, Virginia: Northern Neck Industrial Academy, 1934. (Typewritten.)

Botune, Elizabeth H. First Days Amongst the Contrabands. New York: Arno and the New York Times, 1968.

Bowes, Paul E. "Historical Background of Secondary Education in Fredericksburg, Virginia. " Fredericksburg: Mayfield High School, 1940. (Typewritten.)

Brown, William W. Narrative of the Life of William W. Brown: A Fugitive Slave. The Anti-Slavery Office, 1847.

Caldwell, A. B. History of the American Negro: Virginia Edition. Atlanta: A. B. Caldwell, 1921. 5 vols.

Chambers, Bradford (ed.). Chronicles of Black Protest. New York: New American Library, 1968.

Clayon, Porte. "Our Negro Schools. " Harper's News Monthly Magazine, September 1874.

Corey, Charles H. A History of the Richmond Theological Seminary with Reminiscences of Thirty Years' Work Among the Colored People of the South. Richmond: J. W. Randolph, 1895.

Cubberly, Ellwood P. The History of Education. New York: Houghton Mifflin, 1920.

Dabney, Charles W. Universal Education in the South. Chapel Hill: University of North Carolina Press, 1936; reprint, New York: Arno and the New York Times, 1969. 2 vols.

Dann, Martin E. (ed.). The Black Press: 1827-1890. New York: Capricorn, 1971.

Douglass, Frederick. My Bondage and My Freedom. New York: Miller, Ortigan, and Mulligan, 1855.

_____ . Narrative of the Life of Frederick Douglass, An American Slave. Boston: Published at the Anti-Slavery Office, 1845.

Dubois, W. E. B. The Common School and the Negro American. Atlanta: Atlanta University Press, 1911.

Fisher, Miles Mark. Virginia Union University and Some of Her Achievements. Richmond: Virginia Union University, 1924.

Foner, Philip S. (ed.). W. E. B. Dubois Speaks, 1890-1919. New York: Pathfinder, 1970.

Fortune, Thomas. Black and White: Land, Labor, and Politics in the South. New York: Fords, Howard and Hulbert, 1884.

Goodell, William. The American Slave Code. New York: American and Foreign Anti-Slavery Societies, 1858.

Grant, Jason C. , Sr. Thirty Second Annual Bulletin of Mayfield High School Located at Fredericksburg, Virginia, 1936-1937. Fredericksburg: Charles Carmichael, 1937.

Hartshorn, W. N. An Era of Progress and Promise,
1863-1910; The Religious, Moral and Educational Development
of the Negro Since His Emancipation. Boston: Pricilla, 1910.

Harvey, Watson, R. , Sr. "My Life: Who Am I?"
St. Stephen's Church, Virginia: First Mount Olive Baptist
Church, 1974. (Mimeographed.)

Higgison, Thomas Wentworth. Army Life in a Black
Regiment. Boston: Beacon, 1962.

Leavell, Ullin Whitney. Philanthropy in Negro Education. Nashville, Tennessee: Cullom and Chortner, 1930.

Morehouse, Henry L. Baptist Home Missions in America. New York: George Wheat, 1883.

Morton, Robert Russa. What the Negro Thinks. New
York: Doubleday, Doran, 1929.

Olmsted, Frederick Law. The Cotton Kingdom: A
Traveller's Observation of Cotton and Slavery in the American
Slave States. New York: Mason Brothers, 1861.

_____ . A Journey in the Back Country. New York:
Mason Brothers, 1860.

_____ . A Journey in the Seaboard Slave States with
Remarks on Their Economy. New York: Dix and Edwards,
1856.

_____ . The Slave States. New York: Capricorn,
1959.

Pius, N. H. An Outline of Baptist History. Nashville,
Tennessee: National Baptist Publishing Board, 1911.

Powell, W. H. R. Illustrations from a Supervised Life.
Philadelphia: Continental, 1968.

Ransome, William L. History of the First Baptist
Church, South Richmond. Richmond, Virginia: Publisher
Unknown, 1935.

Rice, Elizabeth C. "A Yankee Teacher in the South,
An Experience in the Early Days of Reconstruction, " Century
Magazine, 62 (May 1901).

Semple, R. B. History of the Rise and Progress of
the Black Baptists of Virginia. Richmond, Virginia: Publisher
Unknown, 1810.

Tate, Joseph. A Digest of the Laws of Virginia.
Richmond, Virginia: Publisher Unknown, 1841.

Wilson, Joseph T. The Black Phalanx: A History of
the Negro Soldiers of the United States in the Wars of 1775-
1812, 1861-1865. Hartford, Connecticut: American, 1890.

Woodson, Carter G. The Education of the Negro Prior
to 1861. Washington, D. C. : The Associated Publishers, 1919;
reprint, New York: Arno and the New York Times, 1968.

_____ . The History of the Negro Church. Washington, D. C. : The Associated Publishers, 1972.

_____. Miseducation of the Negro. Washington,
D. C. : The Associated Publishers, 1933.
_____. The Negro in Our History. Washington,
D. C. : The Associated Publishers, 1922.
Yetman, Norman R. Life Under the Peculiar Institu-
tion. New York: Holt, Rinehart, and Winston, 1970. A
compenidum of slave narratives collected from ex-slaves by
researchers who worked under the auspices of the Federal
Writer's Project, Works Progress Administration, Washing-
ton, D. C.
Young, Andrew P. "Caroline Baptist Sunday School
Union: Revised History, 1922. " Bowling Green, Virginia:
Shiloh Baptist Church, 1922. (Handwritten.)

II.   Secondary Sources

A.   Books

Adams, Russell. Great Negroes: Past and Present.
3d ed. Chicago: Afro-Am, 1969.
Agar, Herbert. Abraham Lincoln. London: Collins,
1953.
Ames, Susie M. Studies of the Virginia Eastern Shore
in the Seventeenth Century. Richmond, Virginia: Dietz, 1940.
Andrews, Sidney. The South Since the War. Boston:
Houghton Mifflin, 1971.
Aptheker, Herbert. And Why Not Every Man? New
York: International, 1970.
_____. Nat Turner's Slave Rebellion, Including the
Full Text of Nat Turner's 1831 "Confession. " New York:
Grove, 1968.
_____. To Be Free. New York: International,
1969.
Baker, Ray Stannard. Following the Color Line: An
Account of Negro Citizenship in the American Democracy.
Williamstown, Massachusetts: Corner House, 1973.
Ballagh, James C. A History of Slavery in Virginia.
Baltimore: Johns Hopkins Press, 1902.
Barnes, Gilbert Hobbs. The Anti-Slavery Impulse:
1830-1844. New York: Harcourt Brace and World, 1964.
Beam, Lura. He Called Them by the Lightening: A
Teacher's Odyssey in the Negro South, 1908-1919. New York:
Bobbs-Merrill, 1967.
Bennett, Lerone, Jr. Before the Mayflower. Balti-
more: Penguin, 1964.

_____. Confrontation: Black and White. Baltimore:
Penguin, 1965.

Bergman, Peter M., and Bergman, Mort N. The
Chronological History of the Negro in America. New York:
New American Library, 1969.

Bertleson, David. The Lazy South. New York: Oxford University Press, 1967.

Billingsley, Andrew. White Families in White America.
Englewood Cliffs, New Jersey: Prentice-Hall, 1968.

Billington, Ray Allen (ed.). The Journal of Charlotte
Forten: A Free Negro in the Slave Era. New York: Collier,
1953.

Blaustein, Albert P. Negro Education in Alabama: A
Study in Cotton and Steel. New York: Atheneum, 1969.

_____, and Zangrando, Robert L. Civil Rights
and the American Negro: A Documentary History. New York:
Washington Square, 1969.

Bontemps, Arna, and Conroy, Jack. Anyplace But Here.
New York: Hill and Wang, 1966.

_____. 100 Years of Negro Freedom. New York:
Dodd, Mead, 1961.

Brawley, Benjamin. Negro Builders and Heroes.
Chapel Hill: University of North Carolina Press, 1965.

Broderick, Francis L., and Meier, August (eds.).
Negro Protest Thought in the Twentieth Century. New York:
Bobbs-Merrill, 1965.

Broom, Leonard, and Glenn, Norval. Transformation
of the Negro American. New York: Harper and Row, 1965.

Brotz, Howard (ed.). Negro Social and Political
Thought: 1850-1920. New York: Basic Books, 1966.

Bruce, Philip A. The Plantation Negro as a Freeman.
Williamstown, Massachusetts: Corner House, 1970.

Bullock, Henry Allen. A History of Negro Education
in the South from 1619 to the Present. Cambridge, Massachusetts: Harvard University Press, 1967.

Butcher, Margaret Just. The Negro in American Culture. New York: New American Library, 1956.

Carpenter, J. T. The South as a Conscious Minority,
1789-1861. New York: New York University Press, 1930

Cash, W. J. The Mind of the South. New York:
Vintage, 1960.

Channing, Steven A. Crisis of Fear: Secession in
South Carolina. New York: Simon and Schuster, 1970.

Clark, Kenneth. Dark Ghetto: Dilemma of Social
Power. New York: Harper and Row, 1965.

Cronon, E. David. Black Moses: The Story of Marcus Garvey and the Universal Negro Improvement Association.
Madison: University of Wisconsin Press, 1955.

Current, Richard N. (ed.). Reconstruction: 1865-
1877. Englewood Cliffs, New Jersey: Prentice-Hall, 1965.
Current, Richard N. (ed.); Williams, T. Harry; and
Freidel, Frank. American History. New York: Knopf, 1966.
Daniel, Pete. The Shadow of Slavery: Peonage in the
South, 1901-1969. New York: Oxford University Press, 1973.
Dennett, Richard. The South as It Is: 1865-1866.
New York: Viking, 1965.
Dobler, Lavinia, and Toppin, Edgar A. Pioneers and
Patriots. New York: Zenith, 1965.
Douglass, Frederick. Life and Times of Frederick
Douglass. New York, Collier, 1971.
Drimmer, Melvin (ed.). Black History: A Reappraisal.
Garden City, New York: Doubleday, 1968.
Dubois, W. E. B. The Gift of Black Folk: The Ne-
groes in the Making of America. New York: Washington
Square, 1970.
_____. The Negro Church. Atlanta: Atlanta Uni-
versity Press, 1903.
_____. The Souls of Black Folk. New York: Faw-
cett, 1968.
Dupuy, R. Ernest, and Dupuy, Trevor N. The Com-
pact History of the Civil War. New York: Collier, 1962.
Eaton, Clement. The Growth of Southern Civilization.
New York: Harper and Row, 1965.
Edwards, G. Franklin. E. Franklin Frazier on Race
Relations. Chicago: University of Chicago Press, 1969.
Elkins, Stanley M. Slavery: A Problem in American
Institutional and Intellectual Life. New York: Grosset and
Dunlap, 1959.
Eppse, Merl R. The Negro Too, in American History.
Nashville, Tennessee: National, 1943.
Feldstein, Stanley. The Poisoned Tongue: A Docu-
mentary History of American Racism and Prejudice. New
York: William Morrow, 1972.
Fine, Sidney, and Brown, Gerlads. The American
Past: Conflicting Interpretations of the Great Issues. New
York: Macmillan, 1961. 2 vols.
Fisher, Miles Mark. Negro Slave Songs in the United
States. Citadel, 1963.
Foster, William Z. The Negro People in American
History. New York: International, 1973.
Franklin, John Hope. From Slavery to Freedom: A
History of Negro Americans. New York: Knopf, 1947.
_____. The Militant South, 1800-1861. Cambridge,
Massachusetts: Belknap Press of Harvard University Press,
1956.

_____. Reconstruction After the Civil War. Chicago: University of Chicago Press, 1961.

_____, and Starr, Isidore (eds.). The Negro in Twentieth Century America. New York: Vintage, 1967.

Frazier, E. Franklin. Black Bourgeoisie. London: Collier-Macmillan Canada, 1969.

_____. The Negro Church in America. New York: Schocken, 1963.

_____. The Negro Family in the United States. Chicago: University of Chicago Press, 1966.

Freedman, Morris, and Banks, Carolyn. American Mix: The Minority Experience in America. New York: Lippincott, 1972.

Freyre, Gilberto. The Master and the Slave. New York: Knopf, 1946.

Fromm, Erich. Escape from Freedom. New York: William Sloane, 1956.

Genovese, Eugene D. The Political Economy of Slavery. New York: Random House, 1965.

Ginzberg, Eli, and Eichner, Alfred S. The Troublesome Presence: American Democracy and the Negro. New York: New American Library, 1966.

Graham, Hugh Davis, and Gurr, T. Robert. The History of Violence in America. New York: Bantam, 1969.

Grant, Joanne, Black Protest: History, Document, and Analyses, 1619 to the Present. Greenwich, Connecticut: Fawcett, 1968.

Hamilton, Charles V. The Black Preacher in America. New York: Morrow, 1972.

Handlin, Oscar. Race and Nationality in American Life. Garden City, New York: Doubleday Anchor, 1957.

Hawk, Emory Q. Economic History of the South. Englewood Cliffs, New Jersey: Prentice-Hall, 1934.

Herskovits, Melville J. The Myth of the Negro Past. New York: Harper and Brothers, 1941.

Hicks, John D. A History of the United States. Boston: Houghton Mifflin, 1957.

_____. A Short History of American Democracy. New York: Houghton Mifflin, 1943.

Holte, Clarence. Education of Blacks in America: A Brief History. Norfolk, Virginia: Journal and Guide Publishing Co. , 1974.

Hoover, Dwight W. (ed.). Understanding Negro History. Chicago: Quadrangle, 1968.

Hornsby, Alton, Jr. The Black Almanac. Woodbury, New York: Barron's Educational Series, 1973.

Hughes, Langston. Fight for Freedom: The Story of the NAACP. New York: Norton, 1962.

Jackson, Luther Porter. Free Negro Labor and Property Holding in Virginia, 1830-1860. New York: Atheneum, 1969.

Jacobs, Paul; Landau, Saul; and Pell, Eve. To Serve the Devil. New York: Vintage, 1971. 2 vols.

Johnson, Edward A. Johnson's History of the Negro Race. Raleigh, North Carolina: Edwards and Broughton, 1894.

Jones, Edward A. A Candle in the Dark. Valley Forge, Pennsylvania: Judson, 1967.

Jordan, Winthrop D. The White Man's Burden. New York: Oxford University Press, 1974.

Kalven, Harry, Jr. The Negro and the First Amendment. Chicago: University of Chicago Press, 1966.

Katz, Michael. Class Bureaucracy, and School: The Illusion of Educational Change in America. New York: Praeger, 1971.

_____. The Irony of Early School Reform: Educational Innovation in Mid-Nineteenth Century Massachusetts. Cambridge, Massachusetts: Harvard University Press, 1968.

Katz, William Lorenz. Eyewitness: The Negro in American History. New York: Putnam Publishing Corporation, 1968.

Killens, John Oliver. Black Man's Burden. New York: Simon and Schuster, 1970.

Knight, Edgar W. The Academy Movement in the South. Chapel Hill: University of North Carolina Press, 1923.

_____. Public Education in the South. New York: Ginn, 1922.

Knight, Wallace. The Influence of Reconstruction on Education in the South. New York: Teachers College, Columbia University, 1913.

Lacy, Dan. The White Use of Blacks in America. New York: McGraw-Hill, 1973.

Lawrence, Paul; Randall, Florence; Endo, Takako; and McStay, Esther. Negro American Heritage. San Francisco: Century Communications, 1968.

Lee, Guy Carleton. The True History of the Civil War. Philadelphia: Lippincott, 1903.

Leech, Margaret. Reveille in Washington, 1860-1865. New York: Grosset and Dunlap, 1941.

Lincoln, Eric C. The Negro Pilgrimage in America. New York: Bantam, 1967.

Lindenmeyer, Otto. Of Black America, Black History: Lost, Stolen, or Strayed. New York: Avon, 1970.

Lloyd, Arthur. The Slavery Controversy, 1830-1860. Chapel Hill: University of North Carolina Press, 1939.

Logan, Rayford W. The Betrayal of the Negro from
Rutherford B. Hayes to Woodrow Wilson. New York: Col-
lier, 1965.
    Lomax, Louis. The Negro Revolt. New York: New
American Library, 1963.
    Lyman, Stanford M. The Black American in Socio-
logical Thought: A Failure of Perspective. Capricorn, 1973.
    McPherson, James M. The Negro's Civil War: How
American Negroes Felt and Acted During the War for the
Union. New York: Vintage, 1965.
    Makielski, S. J. , Jr. Beleaguered Minorities: Cul-
tural Politics in America. San Francisco: Freeman, 1973.
    Meier, August, and Rudwick, Elliott. From Plantation
to Ghetto. New York: Hill and Wang, 1970.
    _____ and _____. The Making of Black Amer-
ica. New York: Atheneum, 1973. 2 vols.
    Metcalf, George R. Black Profiles. New York:
McGraw-Hill, 1970.
    Meyer, Adolphe. An Educational History of the Amer-
ican People. New York: McGraw-Hill, 1967.
    Mitchell, Paul (ed.). Race Riots in Black and White.
Englewood Cliffs, New Jersey: Prentice-Hall, 1970.
    Moon, Henry Lee (ed.). The Emerging Thought of
W. E. B. Dubois. New York: Simon and Schuster, 1972.
    Moton, Robert Russa. Finding a Way Out: An Auto-
biography. Garden City, New York: Doubleday, Page, 1920.
    Mullen, Robert W. Blacks in America's Wars. New
York: Monad, 1973.
    Myers, Gustavus. History of Bigotry in the United
States. New York: Capricorn, 1960.
    Nichols, Jeannette P. , and Nichols, Roy F. The
Growth of American Democracy. New York: Appleton-
Century, 1939.
    Oates, Stephen. To Purge This Land with Blood.
New York: Harper and Row, 1970.
    Osofsky, Gilbert. The Burden of Race. New York:
Harper and Row, 1967.
    Owsley, Frank Lawrence. Plain People of the Old
South. Baton Rouge: Louisiana State University Press, 1949.
    Paerington, Vernon Louis. Main Currents in Ameri-
can Thought. New York: Harcourt Brace, 1954. 3 vols.
    Pascoe, C. F. Two Hundred Years of the S. P. G. :
An Historical Account of the Society for the Propagation of
the Gospel in Foreign Parts. London: At the Society's Of-
fice, 1901.
    Peabody, Francis Greenwood. Education for Life:
The Story of Hampton Institute. Garden City, New York:
Doubleday, Page, 1926.

178   Black Baptist Schools in Virginia

Pettigrew, Thomas F. A Profile of the Negro Ameri-
can. Princeton, New Jersey: Van Nostrand, 1964.
Phillips, Ulrich B. American Negro Slavery. Baton
Rouge: Louisiana State University, 1918.
_____. Life and Labor in the Old South. New
York: Grosset and Dunlap, 1939.
Ploski, Harry A., and Brown, Roscoe, Jr. The
Negro Almanac. New York: Bellwether, 1967.
Quarles, Benjamin. The Negro in the American
Revolution. Chapel Hill: University of North Carolina Press,
1961.
_____. The Negro in the Civil War. Boston:
Little, Brown, 1969.
_____. The Negro in the Making of America. New
York: Collier, 1968.
Reimes, David M. White Protestantism and the Negro.
New York: Oxford University Press, 1965.
Rhodes, James F. History of the United States. New
York: Macmillan, 1906.
Roberts, J. Deotis. Liberation and Reconciliation:
A Black Theology. Philadelphia: Westminster, 1966.
Rogers, J. A. World's Great Men of Color. New
York: Collier, 1972. 2 vols.
Rose, Arnold. The Negro in America. Boston:
Beacon, 1956.
Russell, John H. The Free Negro in Virginia, 1619-
1865. New York: Dover, 1969.
Schwebel, Milton. Who Can Be Educated? New York:
Grove, 1968.
Shimahara, Nobuo Kenneth, and Scrupski, Adam. So-
cial Forces and Schooling: An Anthropological and Sociolog-
ical Perspective. New York: McKay, 1975.
Silberman, Charles E. Crisis in Black and White.
New York: Vintage, 1964.
Singletary, Otis A. Negro Militia and Reconstruction.
New York: McGraw-Hill, 1963.
Smith, Bob. They Closed Their Schools. Chapel Hill:
University of North Carolina Press, 1965.
Sowell, Thomas. Black Education: Myths and Trage-
dies. New York: McKay, 1973.
Spencer, Samuel R. Booker T. Washington and the
Negro's Place in American Life. Boston: Little, Brown,
1955.
Stampp, Kenneth M. The Peculiar Institution. New
York: Knopf, 1956.
Stephenson, Wendell H. The South Lives in History.
Baton Rouge: Louisiana State University, 1955.

Bibliography 179

Stevens, Charles Emery. Anthony Burns: A History. Williamstown, Massachusetts: Corner House, 1973.

Swint, Henry Lee. The Northern Teacher in the South, 1862-1870. New York: Octagon, 1967.

Thompson, Edgar T. (ed.). Race Relations and the Race Problem. Durham, North Carolina: Duke University Press, 1939.

Thornbrough, Emma Lou (ed.). Black Reconstructionists: Great Lives Observed: Booker T. Washington. Englewood Cliffs, New Jersey: Prentice-Hall, 1969.

Thwing, Charles F. A History of Higher Education in America. New York: Appleton-Century, 1906.

Toppin, Edgar A. A Biographical History of Blacks in America Since 1528. New York: McKay, 1971.

Torrence, Ridgely. The Story of John Hope. New York: Macmillan, 1948.

Tragle, Henry Irving. The Southampton Slave Revolt of 1831. New York: Vintage, 1973.

Twombly, Robert C. Blacks in White America Since 1865: Issues and Interpretations. New York: McKay, 1971.

Warren, Robert Penn. Who Speaks for the Negro? New York: Vintage, 1966.

Weatherford, W. D. American Churches and the Negro. Boston: Christopher, 1857.

Welsch, Ervin K. The Negro in the United States: A Research Guide. Bloomington: Indiana University Press, 1965.

Wish, Henry (ed.). Slavery in the South. New York: Noonday, 1964.

Woodward, C. Vann. The Strange Career of Jim Crow. New York: Oxford University Press, 1974.

Yette, Samuel F. The Choice: The Issue of Black Survival in America. New York: Putnam's, 1972.

B. Articles

Aptheker, Herbert. "Black Studies and United States History," Negro History Bulletin 34 no. 8 (December 1971): 174-177.

Bond, Horace Mann. "Social and Economic Forces in Alabama Reconstruction," Journal of Negro History 23 no. 2 (July 1938): 290-348.

Craven Avery O. "The Turner Theories and the South," Journal of Southern History 5 (August 1939): 291-314.

Daniel, W. Harrison. "Virginia Baptists and the Negro in the Antebellum Era," Journal of Negro History 56 no. 1 (January 1971): 1-17.

Dubois, W. E. B. "Reconstruction and Its Benefits," American Historical Review 15 (July 1910): 781-799.

Hofstadter, Richard. "U. B. Phillips and the Plantation Legend," Journal of Negro History 29 (April 1944): 109-124.

Kimball, William J. "The Gabriel Insurrection of 1800," Negro History Bulletin 34 no. 7 (November 1971): 153-157.

Lovell, John. "The Social Implications of the Negro Spirituals," Journal of Negro Education 8 (1939): 634-643.

McLean, Helen V. "The Emotional Health of Negroes," Journal of Negro Education 18 (Summer 1949): 283-290.

Meyers, I. A. "A Study of Anti-Negro Prejudice," Journal of Negro Education 12 (1943): 709-714.

Parmet, Robert D. "Schools for the Freedman," Negro History Bulletin 34 no. 6 (October 1971): 128-133.

Parrish, C. H. "Color Names and Color Notions," Journal of Negro Education 15 (1946): 13-20.

Pease, William H. "Three Years Among the Freedmen: William C. Gannett and the Port Royal Experiments," Journal of Negro History 62 (April 1957): 98-117.

Pope, Liston. "The Negro Religion in America," Review of Religion Research 5 no. 3 (Spring 1964): 142-152.

Quarles, Benjamin. "Founding Peoples and Immigrants: A Black Bicentennial Perspective," Chisis 82 (August-September 1975): 244-249.

Sio, Arnold A. "Interpretations of Slavery: The Slave States in the Americas," Comparative Studies in Society and History 7 (April 1965): 289-308.

Smith, Robert P. "William Cooper Nell: Crusading Black Abolitionist," Journal of Negro History 55 no. 3 (July 1970): 182-200.

Stampp, Kenneth. "The Historian and Southern Negro Slavery," American Historical Review 57 (April 1952): 613-634.

Suttles, William C., Jr. "African Religious Survivals and Factors in American Slave Revolts," Journal of Negro History 56 no. 2 (April 1971): 97-105.

Sydnor, Charles S. "The Southerner and the Laws," Journal of Southern History 6 (February 1940): 3-23.

Turner, W. Burghardt. "Joel Augustus Rogers: An Afro-American Historian," Negro History Bulletin 35 no. 2 (February 1972): 34-40.

Wesley, Charles H. "Racism and Voting," Negro History Bulletin 35 (May 1972): 100-103.

C. Unpublished Theses and Dissertations.

Albanese, Anthony Gerald. "The Plantation as a School: The Sea Islands of Georgia and South Carolina, A Test Case, 1800-1860. " Doctorate of Education dissertation, Rutgers University, New Brunswick, New Jersey, 1970.

Lewis, Frank P. "A History of the Baptist General Association of Virginia (Colored). " Bachelor of Divinity thesis, Virginia Union University, Richmond, Virginia, 1937.

Thompson, Samuel M. "The Influence of the Baptist Church Upon the Education of the Negro in Virginia. " Master of Science thesis, Virginia State College, Petersburg, Virginia, 1945.

D. Interviews

Booker, Sylvester C. Richmond, Virginia. Interview, January 8, 1975.

Brown, Evelyn Collins. Richmond, Virginia. Interview, January 10, 1975.

Downing, George E. Newark, New Jersey. Interview, September 18, 1975.

Ellison, John M. Virginia Union University, Richmond, Virginia. Interview, January 9-12, 1975.

Johnson, General. Richmond, Virginia. Interview, January 11-12, 1975.

Jones, Mary B. Indian Neck, Virginia. Interview, January 21, 1975.

Lewis, Frank P. Lynchburg, Virginia. Interview, January 10, 1975.

Ransome, W. L. Richmond, Virginia. Interview, January 11, 1975.

Russell, Wendell P. Federal City College, Washington, D. C. Interview, February 1975.

Young, Andrew P. Bowling Green, Virginia. Interview, January 12, 1975.

NAME INDEX

A

Abbott, A. R.   158
Abbott, Sylvia   162
Allen, J. C.   65
Allen, T. M.   86, 129
Alsop, William   69
Anderson, Annie   162
Armistead, J. M.   146
Armistead, William   6
Arnold, Benedict   6

B

Bacoates, John A.   94
Ball, Mrs. Ella Smith   74
Ball, Levi R.   70-71, 74,
   119, 147
Banks, Robert J.   130
Barco, H. L.   58, 146
Barton, Judge,   160
Bass, Henry   101
Bates, J. H.   86
Baylor, James   127-129
Baylor, Nettie   130
Baylor, Victoria   130
Beasley, Mark   129
Beecher, James   137
Benn, Herbert   101
Berry, Cora P.   130
Berry, Delegate   16
Beverly, J. M.   129
Binga, Anthony   35, 150
Binney, J. G.   23, 42, 44

Bishop, Josiah   10
Blue, G. W.   76
Booker, Sylvester   73-75
Booth, J. W.   150
Bowes, Douglas   97
Bowes, Frederick D.   97-
   98, 161
Bowes, Paul E.   95, 97
Bowler, Jack   11
Bowler, William   134
Bowling, Richard   55, 147
Boxley, George   12
Brooks, Nancy   67
Brown, Clementine   93
Brown, Douglas   163
Brown, Evelyn C.   63-65
Brown, J. E.   91-92
Brown, John   20
Brown, Louise   162
Brown, Marie   162
Brown, Samuel   91-92
Bruce   100
Buchanan, G. J.   87-88,
   130
Burton, M. L.   83
Butler, Benjamin   20
Butler, Geneva   162
Byrd, J. R.   130
Byrd, Rosa T.   132

C

Carey, Lott   14
Cauthorn, George   66

Green, Mrs. Henry   74
Green, James   69
Griffin, Lucille   162
Grimes, Leonard A.   17
Guss, E. L. R.   130

H

Hailstalk, John   158
Hailstalk, L. E.   158
Hailstalk, Lucretia   158
Hairston, Luvenia   162
Haislip   160
Hall, W. T.   146
Hamilton   90
Hamn, Arthur   162
Hardman, Thomas   132
Hardy, R. B.   150
Harrell, J. A.   99-100
Harris, Bessie   162
Harrison, Lucille   162
Hartshorn, Joseph C.   48
Harvey, Watson R.   65-69
Hayes, Gregory W.   52-56,
   140-143, 146, 148
Hayes, Mrs. Mary Rice   56
Hayes, William H.   75
Henderson, Ada   162
Henderson, H. M.   102-103
Henderson, John M.   47, 100
Henderson, Thomas   47
Hester, B. H.   94-95
Higginson, T. W.   137
Hill, R. T.   147
Hill, Richard R.   29
Hoffman, Jerry   81
Hoffman, R. T.   146
Holmes, Booker T.   82
Holmes, James   35, 149
Holmes, Samuel B.   68,
   89-90
Hovey, George R.   77
Howard, James   162
Howard, O. O.   32
Howe, Lewis   144
Hudson, Adoniram   21

Huskeron, William A.   100-
   101

J

Jackson, Ella   162
Jackson, Jeanette   163
Jackson, Louise   163
Jacox, David G.   145
James, Allex   47
Jefferson, Thomas   7
Johns, Vernon   56
Johnson, Andrew   28-29,
   39-40
Johnson, E. A.   86, 129
Johnson, General   80-81
Johnson, Georgia   163
Johnson, Harvey   146
Johnson, Maggie   130
Johnson, Martha Ellen   66
Johnson, S. L.   75
Johnson, Thomas   100
Johnson, W. T.   144
Johnson, Walter   163
Jones, J. E.   56
Jones, Lea   68
Jones, Mary B.   107-108,
   110
Jones, Thomas Jesse   74-
   75, 78, 83, 99
Joynes, Henry   65

K

Katz, Michael   2, 27, 33,
   107
Kennedy, John F.   47
King, George M. P.   65
Kirby, J. W.   145

L

Lafayette, Marquis De   6
Lambeth   4

U

Upshaw, Maggie   128

V

Vann, Fred   101
Vaughan, Elizabeth   132
Vick, G. L.   95

W

Walker, A. M.   88, 131
Walker, Joseph A.   91-92,
   97-98, 160-161
Washington, Allen   163
Washington, Booker T.   62
Washington, Bushrade   13
Washington, George   13
Washington, John   87, 130
Washington, Lizzie B.   132
Watts, Doris   163
Watts, E.   150
Watts, Lloyd   163
Wells, Aaron   46
Wells, Richard   35, 149-
   150
Wheeler, Elizabeth   163
White, Albert   69
White, Randolph   82
Whiteley, P. C.   92-93
Williams, Addie   163
Williams, Douglas   145-146
Williams, Henry   145-146
Williams, Mary   163
Willis, Gladys   163
Willis, S. G.   91
Wilson, J. H.   75
Wilson, Leah Marie   62
Wilson, U. G.   62-64
Winston, D. C.   89, 129
Winston, Leslie   89
Wood, R. C.   56
Woolfolk, Peter   36
Wright, Frances E.   87-88,

130-131, 133
Wright, Grant   97
Wright, J. Early   102
Wright, Montgomery   127
Wright, Naomi   97
Wright, Rebecca   84

X

Xavier, Francis   21

Y

Yates, Naomi   163
Yerby, W. D.   74
Young, A. P.   68, 88,
   127, 130
Young, Carrie   130
Young, Daisy   132
Young, Elkanah   130
Young, Gertrude   88, 131
Young, Hovey R.   88, 131
Young, James B.   132
Young, Mary   130
Young, Randolph W.   85-86,
   128-129
Young, Stephen R.   130
Young, Viola   130
Young, W. A.   81-82
Young, W. G.   86
Young, W. J.   86, 129
Young, W. L.   128, 131
Young, Wilson C.   86, 127,
   129

SUBJECT INDEX

A

Abyssinian Baptist Church, New York City   10, 47, 97
Accomac County, Va.   4, 63
Africa   13-14, 24, 46, 103
African Baptist Church, Richmond, Va.   17
Agreement of 1896 made at Norfolk, Va.   54, 107, 151
Agriculture and Technical College, Greensboro, N. C.   47
Alabama   106
Alexandria, Va.   41, 50, 57
Amelia County, Va.   52
American Baptist Home Mission Society   32, 39, 42, 44-45,
    49, 51-55, 57-58, 64-65, 105-107; Elementary School,
    Owenton, Va.   65; Fifty-First Annual Session   45
American Baptist Publication Society   57
American Colonization Society   13-15
American Dream   106
American Missionary Association   22, 105
Angel Visit Baptist Church, Ozeana, Va.   79-80
Antioch Baptist Church, Mathews, Va.   102
Apprenticeship System   2, 6
Atlanta, Ga.   44
Atlanta University, Atlanta, Ga.   32

B

Baltimore, Md.   74
Bank-Street Baptist Church, Norfolk, Va.   47, 103
Bannister Baptist Association, Houston, Va.   58, 77-78
Baptist General Association of Virginia (Colored)   49, 56,
    58-61, 64, 72, 78, 82-84, 93-94, 101-103
Baptist General Association of Virginia (White)   57
Baptist General Convention of Virginia   57, 60
Baptist Women's Convention, Virginia   79

M

Maggie Walker High School, Richmond, Va.   82
Maine   32
Manchester, Va.   35
Maryland   63, 67
Massachusetts   28
Mathews County, Va.   102
Mayfield, Va.   92-95
Mayfield High School, Fredericksburg, Va.   93-95, 97-98,
   107
Meherrin, Va.   76
Methodists   8, 105
Middlesex County, Va.   66, 68, 79, 81
Milford, Va.   85
Ministers, Black   17, 22, 24, 35
Mission Monthly Magazine   53-54
Missionaries   1, 22, 27, 33, 43
Mississippi   39, 106
Mount Hope Baptist Church, Brooke, Va.   91-92, 94
Mount Tabor Baptist Church, Caroline County, Va.   86-87
Mount Zion Baptist Church, Richmond, Va.   58

N

Nansemond Collegiate Institute, Suffolk, Va.   41, 98-101
Nansemond County, Va.   98-99
Nansemond County Training School for Blacks, Suffolk, Va.
   101
Nansemond Institute, Suffolk, Va.   98-101
Nat Turner Insurrection   104
National Association for the Advancement of Colored People
   72
National Era   7-15
National Theological Institute and University, Washington,
   D. C.   43-44
New Brunswick, New Jersey   47
New Jersey   47, 60, 65, 67
New Kent County, Va.   6
New Morning Star Baptist Church, St. Stephens Church, Va.
   66
New York   101
New York City   10, 22, 45, 47, 74, 97
Newport News, Va.   22, 97
Newtown, Va.   69
Norfolk, Va.   11-12, 16-17, 49, 54